An
Exodus
for
Hope

First Edition: September 2010

An Exodus for Hope: the footsteps of a dream

15206 18th Ave, W Lynnwood, WA 98087
Tel: 425-745-9977

ISBN 978-89-01-11245-9
CIP 2010003028
A CIP catalogue record for this book is available from the e-CIP center of the National Library of Korea(http://www.nl.go.kr/ecip)

Printed in South of Korea
Edited by Daniel Yongsung Lee

the story of Paull H. Shin

An Exodus for Hope

the footsteps of a dream...

WJ JISIKHOUSE

jOurney

A past denied, now accepted.

Exposing truths, now public domain.

No longer burdened by shame or embarrassment,

I took the liberty of discovering freedom through expression.

Not to be judged or scrutinized,

Not to boast or criticize,

But as a message of hope and encouragement.

If my testimony serves as inspiration

To a single soul,

Withered and defeated by the disappointments of life,

I willingly reveal

Till I stand exposed.

Inadequacies elucidate

Under an incandescent glare.

But sympathizing tears and reassuring smiles,

Comforting whispers and brightening ideas,

Blanket the midnight sky

And restore confidence in my ability to matter.

I take this opportunity to recognize all
Who supported me through failures and joined in my victories.
Above all, I glorify God.
He kept His arms open, heart available and eyes fixed,
For over sixty years.
He continues to promise endless abundance.
Amidst uncertainties God remains constant,
Whether I acknowledge or deny,
His deliberate provision.

Words mobilized my dormant past,
But words cannot describe my appreciation,
For all the love I've received and wish to share.
I visualized many dreams, I imagined many fantasies,
But I never expected to embrace these dreams in reality.
I imagine still, I dream always,
I anticipate many more opportunities to revive distant fantasies.

PROLOGUE

Undeserving and a little apprehensive, I open up past wounds to share personal experiences. I do not presume to revel in my own glory or boast my successes.

This is one man's journey transplanting from one culture to another. Confusion and ambiguity threatened, but I found certainty by accepting adversity. Deprivation was my excuse for desire, and hope, my motivation to achieve.

I started at the bottom of the "social ladder", but started to climb by rebuilding the structure. I started alone, but many people stumbled upon my path and helped me along. If I followed the designs of society I would have remained where I started, but the trauma of discrimination, and a search for my identity pushed me beyond my comfort zone.

The Korean War, for most Koreans, marks a time of tragedy

and loss. I share sympathetic feelings, but cannot ignore the opportunities that the war opened for me. Because of the war, I met an American soldier who gave me a home in his, and extended his love to me. In America I started from my ABC's to take the GED and earned a PhD.

One at a time, I started to actualize my dreams, and made a habit out of overcoming obstacles. In the end, I found something to offer: my story. Through it, I hope people learn they have a lot more to volunteer.

Paull H. Shin

In loving memory of Ray Paull,
He extended his compassion to all he met,
Even a boy from Korea
Who had nothing to offer in return.
I called him *"Father"*.

CONTENTS

Sharing a Dream

i coun**t**ed the stars...

Because I was so hungry, I counted the stars.
Longing for my mother, I wondered at the stars.

On sleepless nights, I looked to the stars.
When I felt so alone, I found friendship in the stars.

With nothing to hope for, I reached for the stars.
Feeling so small, I measured the stars.

Each star I discovered,
Gave me hope for tomorrow.
Stepping beyond reality,
Surrounded by their light,
I keep counting the stars.

Unattainable Dreams

my mother went over the mountain

"*Ahn young, ahn young,*" (Hello, hello)

"*Mung mung, ahn young,*" (Doggie, hello)

"*Nahmoo, ahn young,*" (Tree, hello)

Perched on my grandmother's back, I practiced my limited vocabulary as we walked to the house where my mom was renting a small room. At the house, my grandmother pushed open the picket fence and called out softly, "Hobom's here." She didn't want to disturb the landlord.

The door of a room struggled to open, and my mother weakly looked out.

"Come in, come in! Mother, thank you for bringing Hobom." She tried to look and sound healthy, but her effort was unconvincing.

"How are you feeling today?" my grandmother asked.

"I'm fine. I just wish I could be of some help to you instead of being such a burden."

"I told you not to worry about me. Think about your child and concentrate on getting well."

"I'm so sorry…"

My mother never got better. She just grew weaker and weaker until one day I walked into the courtyard holding my aunt's hand to find some men building a wooden box. Even as a four-year-old, I could feel the unease and sympathy in the way people looked at me. I began looking for my grandmother.

"Grandma, Grandma! Where's Mom? Where did she go?" Her answer was so choked up by tears that I couldn't understand her. I just tugged harder at her skirt.

"Mommy, where are you?"

"Your mom went over the mountain!"

"Tell her to come back!"

"I'm so sorry. My poor child. What are we going to do?"

For the next few days I continued to ask for my mother, and each time my grandmother gave me the same answer, "Your mom can't come back! We buried her in the ground on the other side of the mountain!"

"I want you to take me to her. I'll get a shovel and dig her out!"

I whined and threw tantrums for days, but nobody brought my mom back.

My mother left my father a young widower, incapable of raising a four-year-old boy. He left me in my grandmother's care and disappeared.

I entered the world in September of 1935, in Geumchon, a quiet town in the city of Paju, Gyeonggi Province, Korea. I was born as the first son to Kwangsung Shin and Insung Kang.

As a small country situated in a very vulnerable and convenient location, Korea constantly fell victim to greater powers surrounding the peninsula.

In 1905, Japan forced Korea to sign a protectorate treaty, and finally annexed the nation in 1910. Although greater incentives lie in mainland China, Korea attracted Japan's imperialistic ambition and performed as a bridge to extending the empire. Forcing most of the produce back to Japan left Korea, a predominantly agricultural society, hungry and defenseless.

Land ownership remained in the hands of the educated, upper-class elite known as the *yangban*, and the majority of the population survived as tenant farmers or sharecroppers. Although poor, my father was a highly valued farmhand, not only because of his physical strength, but also because of his loyalty and compassion. Villagers looked up to him and knew to call on him to pull out the ox cart stuck in a creek or to do anything that required extraordinary strength. He was a third generation tenant farmer, held prisoner by poverty. My father's family accepted their lives as tenant farmers and sharecroppers, or sold their strength for manual labor. Most of the country folks dreamed of traveling to the city as merchants, but without an education, this dream remained a dream—

unattainable.

My mother was tall for a Korean woman. Despite her height, she was a paragon of "Asian" beauty with a slender figure and delicate features. As the daughter of an educated father and a hard-working mother, she was considered well-off for her time. But she fell in love with a poor man and left her relatively privileged life to live with her husband in a small, rented room. Fearing misfortune, the superstitious owners would not allow my mother to give birth in their new home before them, so I entered the world on the cold, dirt floor of their kitchen which was separated from the main house.

On the border of the 38th parallel in between Ilsan and Munsan, lies Geumchon. We lived on the outskirts of Geumchon, about 40 minutes by foot from the train station, but no buses to accommodate the distance because there were only fifty some cottages scattered throughout the countryside. To the east of the village was more farmland, and at the end of the horizon was the town of Bongilchon. Once a week, a traveling farmer's market stopped there, and on that day, my father always stumbled home, drunk.

I was only a little boy, but I still remember the image of my father staggering home. Only many years later would I understand the reason for his drinking. My mother was diagnosed with breast cancer after she gave birth to me, but his inability to provide proper medical care for his sick wife overwhelmed him with guilt. He couldn't even afford medicine to diminish her pain. He lived each day dreading the next, and hoped that alcohol could bring some consolation. I rarely saw my father. I even avoided him in fright.

My mother was unable to take care of me, so she sent me away on her mother's back, and never knew the joy of nurturing her son. I grew up on rice gruel rather than my mother's milk. My strongest recollection of my mother is of getting into trouble for staining her clothes with pine tree juice. The doctor told me about my mother's condition, but too young to understand the circumstances of my separation, she remained a distant figure, apathetic to her suffering son.

After my mother became sick, my grandmother sent up many prayers for her recovery, but eventually gave up faith in the existence of a compassionate god.

"What crimes did the child commit?" she cried. "How could the heavens be so cruel?"

At my grandmother's house, I lived with my uncle, his wife, and their three children. My grandmother earned her keep by taking care of the children, but I was an unwanted addition, especially after my uncle passed away. Between her field and her family, my aunt already had plenty to worry about without me adding to her burden. Fortunately, many distant relatives lived in the village, so I spent my days wandering from house to house.

I might have had places to go, but I never had enough to eat. Parents struggled to feed their own immediate families, so no one welcomed my company or asked if I was hungry. When I suddenly appeared at mealtimes, everyone cleared the table as if they'd just finished eating. Or if I didn't leave when they needed to set the table, they would ask me, "Don't you have anywhere else to go?" and tactfully nudge me out. If I did happen to eat with them, my portions were always significantly smaller and noticeably watered down.

Whether at home, or visiting a distant relative, I grew up learning how to ignore disapproving glares, and devising ways to avoid the scrutiny of adults. With the lack of adult supervision came freedom. A mutual understanding eliminated reasons to cry or whine about the partiality of my treatment. I must admit I enjoyed a rather spontaneous childhood free from the strict rules and regulations that other children endured.

who told me

Who told me
When people died, they became a star?
That big, bright star,
Could that be my mom?
To be by her side
I have to become a star.

If my mom was here with me,
I could fall asleep
Wrapped in her arms.
I would tag along while she worked in the fields,
Take a trip to the riverside holding her hand,
And hang onto her neck all the way home.

Who told me
When people die, they become a star?
I'll become a small, bright star,
To find my mom in the sky.
I'll take my place
Wrapped in her arms.

just you wait and see…

The Japanese took advantage of the already scarce natural resources in Korea. Exporting all the trees in the forests and mountains back to Japan left us freezing from a shortage of fuel. Layers of clothing could not prevent the cold from biting through the flesh and gnawing at our bones. As the water in the well turned to stone, so did the villagers' hearts. Tolerance and generosity were also in short supply.

In a place where a clock could not be seen or heard, people kept track of time by the sound of the passing trains, and I felt the empty hours go by with the hollow growls in my stomach.

"How could your mom leave you alone at a time like this?" my grandmother often said.

My poor grandmother was left with the responsibility of taking care of a motherless child. I felt sorry for imposing such a burden on my grandmother, and I wished I could find a solution for myself.

During the year of my sixth birthday, a long winter passed and spring followed, but even as summer approached, no one mentioned sending me to school.

One evening, after an afternoon of wandering around the village, I came home to find my cousins gathered around to enjoy *yeot*, a traditional, hard rice candy. My aunt was using a large wooden bat to divide the pieces and distributing them to her kids.

"Hey, what about me?" I complained. "I want some too!"

I quickly noticed there wasn't enough to go around. On a sudden impulse, I grabbed the piece from my youngest cousin, and gobbled it up at once. Furious, he fell back in a tantrum and burst into tears. When my aunt saw what had happened, she took the bat in her hand and beat me mercilessly till I was black and blue from head to toe.

I ran out of the house crying and refused to return. I lingered outside at dinner time, but I did not have the audacity to go into the house. Once everyone had gone to sleep, however, I crept back home quietly, hungry and sore.

Because I didn't have the courage to go inside the room to sleep, I sat outside gazing at the midnight sky, waiting for my grandmother who had gone out.

"They say my mom left me and went over the mountain, but where could my dad be?"

Stars poured out of the heavens to comfort me as I listened to the frogs croak in unison. They seemed oblivious to the environment around them.

Why am I the only one suffering? I thought. What do I have to do to be treated like other people?

After hours of consideration I came to the conclusion that I had to make a lot of money, and buy lots of my own *yeot*. Then I could share with anyone I wanted.

I never saw my grandmother that night, because I decided to run away before she came home.

I declared my independence at the ripe age of five, but it didn't take long to realize I had nowhere to go. I just started walking until I reached the train station and spent the rest of the night crouched in a corner of the station. Just in case my determination grew weak, I kept repeating to myself, "I'm going to the city to make my own money and buy all the *yeot* I can eat. I can even be a *yeot* salesman!"

The morning rush hour was a bustling mix of students, businessmen and sales women on their way to sell products in the market.

I snuck onto the train, hiding between women who balanced large jars of *gochujang* (red, chili pepper sauce), *kimchi* (pickled cabbage), and other merchandise on their heads. They set the jars on the floor and assumed positions in a comfortable squat. As they sampled each other's recipes, they imagined the many customers who would marvel at their delicious food. I watched them compare flavors and wished they would share some of the food with me.

As the train picked up speed, my uncertainty turned to thrilling expectation.

When the train stopped in Seoul two hours later, I hesitated while everyone else stumbled out, then rushed to join the crowd before the sense of loneliness and fear overwhelmed me. So many people from so many places... No one looked familiar, and no one stopped to help or direct me.

I watched in a daze as others shuffled around on their way to school, work or the market. Then I started to notice other kids with dirty faces, looking abandoned and poor. "They must have come here to make money too!" I assumed, and I didn't feel so alone anymore.

A small group of men in blue uniforms suddenly entered the scene, sending the kids into a frantic stampede. They were the Japanese policemen, who kicked and beat any of the street kids they could grab, in the name of "pest control". I had no personal experience with them yet, but I knew I had to escape. I followed the other children and ran outside the train station to find myself in the middle of a busy day in downtown Seoul. I lingered a bit longer before walking toward the South Gate.

I reached a crowded alley of bumping elbows, overflowing with the aroma of a banquet. I had arrived at the food court of the South Gate Market.

"Here! This is all you get!"

A woman pushed a bowl of noodles and rice in front of me. How did she know I was hungry? I don't know if she assumed I was a child beggar and felt sorry for me, or if she wanted to get rid of me. In any case, I accepted the bowl without hesitation, and practically swallowed it whole—food, sweat, snot, and more. Today, over sixty years later, I can still recall the taste and satisfaction of that meal in my mouth.

As the day faded, tents started to fold, and stores closed one at a time. Life vanished with the crowds, but I wasn't ready to leave the alley just yet. It was the only place I knew in the city. I found a comfortable corner, snuggled up against a folded tent, and released the anxiety that had been building up for the past two days.

Early the next day, the morning frost startled my body, and forced me into a tight cuddle until the sun came out and thawed my frozen body. I rose and reacquainted myself with the market. I felt more alert and aware of my environment than I had the previous day. I noticed that when customers bought food, there were always bits and pieces being thrown away. What customers considered waste, I valued as food. At the end of the day, even the ladies who had shooed me away earlier handed me their leftovers.

Remembering the morning chills, I had kept my eyes open throughout the day for some sort of shelter to sleep in at night. By the time I arrived at a "shelter" against the side of a building, a slumber party was already in progress. There were other homeless children settling in for the night. I claimed a space for myself, and breathed a sigh of relief.

I'm not alone, I thought. They have nowhere else to go either.

I shifted around trying to make myself feel more at home on the cold cement floor, but the thought of my grandmother made me toss another turn. I could almost hear her voice calling my name anxiously. As soon as I started to sniffle, the other kids turned to look at me.

Could their tears be all dry and cried out? Or had they forgotten those they left behind?

After a few days of practice, I stopped waiting around for the charity of others. I learned to swipe cucumbers and radishes from the neat piles while the owner looked away. I even enjoyed the thrill and rush in the face of danger. Every now and then I wasn't quick enough and learned what a good slap felt like. As I began to adjust to the street life, I learned to beg for food and money. I even entertained myself by teasing the Japanese policemen and then running away.

The first time someone threw me some spare change, I felt so rich and powerful that I almost bought a bag of *yeot* and ran home, but I used the money to satisfy my craving for some decent food instead. I found out that the rewards of begging didn't go very far.

Without water to take a bath or even wash my face, my greasy hair stretched out in dirty clumps, my face dripped with grime, and my clothes did not survive very well either. I looked like nothing but a homeless beggar.

I wasn't always successful in acquiring food. I ended some days with an empty hand and an empty stomach. Then I would ravage through the trash to find any remnants of food. Often times, what looked and smelled edible turned rotten in my stomach and almost killed me. Even in the most difficult circumstances, however, I never considered returning home. Was it pride or was I just stubborn? Maybe determination…

Whatever it was, something kept me from giving up, and expecting better luck tomorrow.

I'm going to make lots of money, I told myself. You just wait and see! Just wait till I become a *yeot* salesman! I'll carry home a big box and share it with the whole village!

my bed upon a grave

A more politically correct term for a "beggar" might be a "homeless person", a "vagabond", maybe even a "nomad". Home is where a family lives together—a place for rest and sleep. Without such necessities, how could one be categorized as human? Relaxation can be considered a luxury, but even animals need to sleep for the next day. The average human spends a third of life unconscious of the world around. That's why some people prefer a warm blanket to expensive clothes, and a comfortable bed to an extravagant home.

Some might envy a beggar for their freedom and absence of pressure, but does that mean they're willing to exchange their wealth for the unattached life of a beggar? I don't think so. I would rather suffer from lack of sleep surrounded by luxury.

Since the day I left home, my daily task and inescapable mission was searching for food and a place to sleep. It's easy to imagine the threat of winter. Chased out of ticket lobbies and subway stations, those who fell asleep in unsheltered areas were lucky to wake up. During the rainy seasons, drenched with rain and soaked with depression, I found it hard to move or even exist. Even the summers weren't exactly month long camping trips. One might fantasize about sleeping under the stars, but they forget the mosquitoes in the grass and the morning dew that soaks through clothes.

Knowing the overwhelming probability of surprise attacks by policemen, I might go to the countryside, where they were scarce. If it happened to rain, however, I dealt with the consequences through other penalties: seeking refuge in a chicken coop or cow barn welcomed insects to prey on human blood, and chickens attacked intruders in a vicious attempt to protect their fort.

With everything under consideration, however, I preferred the country to the city. Some folks invited me into their homes and allowed me to stay in the kitchens or a servant's room. While I slept in the kitchens, I always gave into the temptation to help myself to some of the food. Servants felt sorry for me and gave me a corner in their own room, but during the night, lice and fleas from my body relocated onto the cleaner bodies, and repaid my gratitude with a punishment. That eliminated any chance for me to receive an invitation to return, or even the right for me to ask.

Seasons change, and natural disasters come and go, but the one concern that tortured my sleep the most, was the possibility of attack from malicious humans, hungry animals, even evil spirits. I spent each night in fear of the unpredictable, and struggled to fall asleep as I imagined the worst. One night, I remembered something I had heard from an old man.

"If you're too scared to go to sleep, you should try sleeping on a grave. The spirits will protect you."

"What are you talking about? That's the most ridiculous thing I ever heard!" I exclaimed.

"I'm serious!"

"Hey I heard something like that too!"

"Really?"

I had to test the theory.

I found a cemetery and lie down at the foot of a grave. Not only did the soft grass make a comfortable bed, a sense of peace flowed over me. Could the spirits really provide protection?

After my discovery, I visited a cemetery whenever I needed a comfortable night of sleep. This experience helped me understand why people pursued religious beliefs and superstitions.

Most people shudder with unease when they pass by a cemetery, even in broad daylight. But I feel confident and reassured in a cemetery.

Men usually seek ways to elaborate a marriage proposal through romantic "manipulation", but when I found the woman I wanted to spend the rest of my life with, many years later, I took her to a public cemetery to ease my fear as I confessed my love and asked her to marry me.

soul food

I learned where and how to get sleep, but I still had to devise ways to satisfy my hunger. The city crawled with competition and indifference, so I would take trips to the countryside to find sustenance. I looked for homes holding a feast, to blend in with the crowd and join their celebration. Unlike parties in Seoul where only invited guests are allowed, the country homes welcomed anyone desiring to join the festivities. I would find a place for myself, clean all the plates in front of me, and guzzle down the rice wine to the very last drop. When I couldn't stand straight, I would even enjoy a nice nap before continuing on my journey.

Sometimes, I discovered food in front of a grave. I knew the deceased's family left it as an offering for the spirit, but I assumed the spirit understood my hunger, and I breathlessly inhaled it. In the summer, however, unless I wanted to suffer from a stomachache, I always checked to make sure the food was still safe.

In any circumstance, God never fails to supply. The goldfish in the ponds tasted delightful if I boiled them in some water, accompanied by the flavoring I earned from begging. On a potato farm, I always found abandoned potatoes, still slightly covered with dirt. I could not bear the thought of letting such valuable food go to waste.

Frogs throughout the fields worked as my main source of nutrition. As long as I had plenty of frog legs, I didn't desire the tastiest ribs, the juiciest steaks, or the fattest drumstick. If you gently press between the legs until the stomach explodes, you can rip off the legs easily and cook it for a most enjoyable meal! I still took advantage of all my resources throughout the fields. Snakes, mice, even the grasshoppers called my name, asking to be cooked and eaten. Unless it ate me first, I developed an appetite for it.

When the harvest season arrived, food flowed throughout the entire land. From the mountain berries to the vegetables across the fields, and the fruits in the trees, they all belonged to the first person to swallow. I would come across a traveling flea market, and their generosity extended to anyone asking for a free bowl of rice and soup.

But autumn always passed by too quickly, and a time came when I couldn't hear the frogs or grasshoppers. Snow covered the empty fields and clothed the bear branches. I was too young to hunt the deer or rabbits in the mountains, so my only alternative was to go door to door and beg. Judging by the owner's expression, I could tell immediately if I was going to get a hot bowl of rice, a cold bowl of leftovers, a door in my face, or a broom against my bottom. I turned around and ran as soon as I recognized hostility, but I never learned how to avoid the stinging slaps. The hand showed no warning before it was across my face. What could they possibly have against me? Didn't they feel sorry for me?

Winter added an element of hopelessness to a beggar's predicament. But "seek and ye shall find, knock and the door shall be opened," because when I gently reached into a hayloft, I felt the warmth of a mice nest at my fingertips. The next thing I knew, it was frying in my can, letting out a mouth-watering aroma that sent my taste buds wild with expectation. How should I describe the product? That phrase, "mm, mm, finger lickin' good!" comes to mind.

I learned early in life never to waste or complain about food, to respect food, and to accept my food with thanksgiving. When available, I had an extensive variety of exotic foods to choose from, but the one thing I craved, the one thing I lacked, was a nice, warm, home-cooked meal, prepared with tender love and care.

Instead of grieving my deprived childhood, I savor every opportunity to fill my stomach, and struggle to replace the bitter and destitute memories.

study burglar

How do you satisfy human desires or expectations? In the freezing winter, I counted the days till spring, and on a rainy day, I anticipated the sunshine. When my stomach felt neglected, I scrounged for food, and when night fell, I sought out a place to sleep. When I felt the urgent call of nature, I found a nice, quiet corner on the streets to dispose of my excrements. These were tangible aspirations that I found solutions to, but I began to discover that the irrational ambitions outnumbered the rational.

I began to envy the students on their way to school, carrying book bags and dressed in warm clothes. Not because of their clean clothes, or shiny shoes, but because they had the privilege of studying.

I'd picture myself in their shoes as they walked to and from school. However, when the other kids caught me staring wishfully, they'd yell, "Hey! What do you think you're looking at? Get away from here, you beggar!"

Kids chased me away with stones, or beat me in a corner. After a good beating, I counted my bruises and felt my swollen head, but the serious injuries remained hidden under the surface. I didn't know how to heal the wounds caused by the pain of an impossible dream.

One winter day, I gathered enough courage to steal a lesson through the window of a small elementary school. If I concentrated hard enough, I could even pretend that I was sitting at a desk in the heated room. I took out the piece of paper and pencil I found, and started copying what the teacher wrote.

For the few minutes of my transformation, I was so absorbed in the exhilaration of my own fantasy that I didn't even notice the approaching policeman.

"What are you doing?" Startled by the voice, I just started to run.

"Hey! Stop right there! I said stop! You better be hopin' I don't catch you!"

I gathered all my energy to run away, but my short legs couldn't compete with an adult. I slipped on a piece of ice, and the policeman seized the opportunity to throw a burning slap across my face.

"What did you steal?"

"Nothing! I didn't steal anything!"

"Don't lie to me! Why would you run?"

"I'm telling the truth! Please believe me."

"Then show me what you have in your hands."

"I can't…not this…"

He forced the paper and pencil from my grip expecting to find incriminating evidence, but immediately realized his accusations were undeserved. With a sudden change of expression, he sympathetically asked, "Are you hungry?"

Too busy crying to answer, and too exhausted to protest, I followed the policeman's lead. By the time I realized where I was, I felt the steam of a hot bowl of noodle soup tickling my nose.

"You must be cold. Eat your soup while it's still hot."

I wondered why the policeman didn't eat, and I wanted to offer him some of mine, but I never stopped eating long enough to ask. The next day, I tried looking for that officer. I wanted to find him and ask, "Can you slap my other cheek and buy me another bowl of soup."

Fed up with my ignorance, I started to memorize each letter, character, and word through the street signs and littered scraps of newspaper. With the help of older beggars, I developed my own standard for literacy.

My hunger for education inspired me to dream of becoming a teacher. I could no longer be satisfied with just learning, but wanted to share my knowledge with others. For a beggar with no hopes of obtaining a proper education, I pursued a ridiculous fantasy. Because my ultimate dream as a child was to join the kids carrying book bags to school, I set out to become an educator, requiring not just one, but many book bags.

torn musician's dream

I liked to dream and live in my own imagination.

In my dreams, I could eat to my satisfaction, go places my feet couldn't take me, do impossible things, possess everything I desired, and even become whoever or whatever I wished.

On hungry nights I dreamt of a hot pot of soup boiling to perfection. On cold nights, I dreamt that I slept wrapped in a soft, comfortable blanket, lying in front of a warm fire. Of course I realized that no matter how much I imagined, a dream couldn't transform a fantasy into reality. But to feel my grandmother's warmth without the long journey or forfeiting my pride; riding against the wind on a bicycle with a whistle flowing from my lips; stepping into the shoes of a student, wearing a watch, and carrying a book bag; even becoming a teacher, instructing a roomful of students...these were all desires possible through dreams. I felt indebted and grateful to the fleeting moments of pleasure.

As I grew older, I started to feel a more persistent urge to transport my dreams into reality.

Once the temperature grew cold enough to freeze the Han River, everyone gathered around with skates to glide along the surface.

I remembered a time when I watched in confusion as the other village children flaunted their New Year's gifts of colorful clothes, and rode their sleds down the snow-covered hills.

"Why don't I ever get colorful clothes? What makes them so special, or me so different?" I complained.

Children struggling to keep their balance held onto their father's hands, while I watched from a distance, with a tear frozen against my cheeks.

One night, I prepared a small bag and a flashlight, to sneak into the Japanese military storage room my friends had been telling me about. The Japanese soldiers gathered excess materials, and put them in a shed before running out of Korea. They set up barricades all around the shed to prevent anyone from stealing, but nobody stood guard.

I crawled under the barricades and ran into the shed. I paused for a moment to gather my failing courage, convinced myself it was too late to turn back, and proceeded with my mission. When I lit the room, my flashlight revealed a room full of goods. I grabbed as many nails, bulbs and anything else small enough to fit in my bag, and escaped.

As soon as business hours began, I took my merchandise to a

second-hand store, and traded them in for ice-skate blades and rope. I couldn't afford to buy shoes, so I found a wooden board, traced my feet, and cut it out with a saw. After attaching the blade to the board, I hammered some nails into the side to work as anchors for my "laces".

Once I secured the "skates" around my feet, I stumbled onto the ice and slowly started to imitate the movements of other skaters. I became the skater of my dreams.

People around me pointed fingers and laughed out loud. Everybody reacted with a wide-eyed, double-take, and then erupted into uncontrollable laughter. I could ignore the humiliation and embarrassment, but I couldn't ignore the pain of the rope digging into my feet. In reality, this dream lasted only ten minutes because the laces cut off the circulation in my feet, and I needed to take a break every ten minutes.

Despite the hassle, that winter my skates made me the happiest beggar alive.

The ice melted, and my skates became useless, but my ambition grew. This time I crawled in and out of the storage several times before I saved up enough money for a small, used accordion. I inserted my hands in the straps, and every time I pushed and pulled, a glorious sound resonated through my fingertips. As long as I held the accordion in my arms, I felt no hunger or fatigue. The skates allowed me to glide across the ice, but my accordion sent me soaring beyond the horizon. I attempted different melodies, and pretended to have become a famous musician.

However, for the first time in my life, I learned that even

dreams could end tragically.

A few bullies going home from school decided to amuse themselves at my expense. They suddenly ran after me, and confiscated my accordion.

"Wow! What's this? An accordion?"

"That's mine! I bought it! Give it back!!!"

"Hey this is fun! Here you try."

"I want to try too!"

They started to pass it around, as I continued to plead with them.

"Please give it back…"

"You have no right to own an accordion! It doesn't suit your status!"

"PuaHahaha!"

"Throw it over here!"

"Please don't, you're gonna break it!"

"Really? Why don't we find out?"

I tried to hold them back and convince them to reconsider their intentions, but that only provoked their cruelty.

When they grew bored of my accordion, instead of returning it to me, they threw down the instrument and beat it to the ground.

"Please, I'm begging you. Don't break it…leave my accordion alone."

They took my already broken accordion and tore it apart till I was left with nothing more than shreds of a dream.

No matter how happy my accordion had once made me feel,

I never tried to buy another one. It was definitely a possibility, but I couldn't repair my shattered dream. I detested my inability to prevent its demise more than I resented those who crushed my accordion out of pure boredom. If it was a dream I couldn't protect, I didn't deserve to keep it.

i'm alive

As *Chu Suk* drew near, the streets of Seoul filled with busy shoppers and appealing displays of food arrangements. *Chu Suk* is an autumn festival, a kind of Korean thanksgiving when people celebrate their good fortune by eating special foods and dressing up in colorful clothes. I found the extravagance of the festivities unnecessary because the holiday spirits did not promote generosity. The change of season also brought cold weather which kept everyone's hands in their pockets, and froze all desires to help the unfortunate. Colder days naturally meant rough nights and unbearable mornings.

Bored, weak, and cold, I waited for a sunny day to join the other beggars for a communal cleaning. When the weather allowed, beggars gathered around and peeled off our lice infested clothes. We squished the pests, one bug at a time. The blood in our fingertips gave us proof of their death, and the taste of their blood brought the satisfaction of revenge.

My colleagues and I lived each day expecting the worst, but hoping to get lucky. Every year, we anticipated the arrival of spring, only to dread the return of winter.

It was during a particularly difficult time that I met Jaewon. At eight, I was already a proud street kid who refused to carry the tin can that branded my status as a beggar. Jaewon was ten. His two-year advantage made him a cynic, who refused to acknowledge any good in humanity or any beauty in life.

Begging is an intensely competitive occupation that doesn't foster friendship. People in my line of work couldn't afford to keep competitors close, except to stay warm at night. But Jaewon and I allowed ourselves to trust each other, and found refuge in friendship. We shared our existing miseries while anticipating our futures. After a day of begging, we reunited at the train station to enjoy our collection together. As long as we had each other, we never worried about sleeping alone or freezing to death in the night. We comforted and relied on each other, and developed a mutually dependent relationship.

One evening I came back to our usual place at the train station for dinner, but Jaewon was nowhere to be found. When he didn't show up I set out to look for him, and a crowd near the railroad tracks caught my attention. I hurried over to join the excitement, but found the attraction very painful. Jaewon committed suicide by stepping in front of a train. Scattered along the tracks, his dead body was barely recognizable even to me. I broke down in tears beside Jaewon. I had lost my best friend.

I clung to his shredded body begging him to return and not leave me alone. No matter how much I shook him, Jaewon remained limp so I kept hoping that someone would wake me up from the terrible nightmare. I was still grieving over Jaewon's body when the Japanese policemen pushed me aside, picked up his remains and threw him onto the back of a truck. I made a futile effort to stop them and chased after the truck, but in the end I was left to eat the dust of my own devastation.

Once I had time to evaluate the situation, I realized that Jaewon's death was not an accident, but a deliberate suicide. He had talked to me often about the hopelessness of life and his preference for death. He always threatened to commit suicide, but I never expected him to act on it. Realization of his suicide replaced my sorrow with anger and a feeling of betrayal. "You coward!" I cried. "I never knew how pathetic you were!"

Without the initial grief and panic, I felt deserted and abandoned. My disappointment in Jaewon developed into bitterness, and robbed all ability to eat or sleep. What happens to Jaewon now? What about me? How could he leave without telling me first? He was my best friend, my only true friend. He had lost the courage to battle another winter, and had decided to escape the suffering for good...but that's why we had each other!

The more I resented him, the stronger my own will to survive became. Jaewon had killed his own future, but I refused to give up my chance to fulfill my dreams—*our* dreams. I was determined to feel unashamed if I ever met Jaewon again. I wanted to be able to tell him, "I lived a life enough for two—one for you and me."

I decided to return to my grandmother. Loneliness and the hassle of finding a replacement for Jaewon weren't my only reasons for returning. The memory of the extreme hunger and relentless cold of the previous winter made me abandon my pride and hurry home.

Forget about the *yeot* I vowed to bring back! My clothes barely clung to my body, and the worn out strands of straw that surrounded my feet could hardly be considered shoes. I expected to get into trouble for running away and worrying the family, but my mind was so consumed with a desire to live that all other dilemmas paled in comparison.

"Hobom's here! He's come back!" My aunt's announcement exploded from her lips as soon as she realized who I was.

"What?!" I heard my grandmother shout. "Hobom? Did you say, Hobom? He's alive?"

My grandmother stumbled out to witness the miracle of my return.

"Hobom! You came back before I died!"

Her curved back hunched even closer to the ground, but she held onto me, and together, we cried to our satisfaction.

I felt reassured that even my aunt seemed happy to see me. That night, I lie next to my grandmother and felt absolute comfort for the first time since I had run away two years before. I didn't even try to loosen the firm grip she held on my wrist.

Putting personal feelings aside, I understood Jaewon's decision to commit suicide. Unlike Jaewon, I always had a place to call home. But Jaewon had no place to go if things became really desperate. I justified Jaewon's suicide as the result of hopelessness.

I spent the next few days enjoying home-cooked food at regular mealtimes, and sleeping peacefully in warm blankets. I almost forgot about the miseries and uncertainties of life on the streets, but my peace ended with the arrival of a man claiming to be my father, who'd come to take me "home."

Many years later, I would learn that after my mother's death, my father had gone as a servant to another household, leaving me with my grandmother. He then went to Japan to work as a laborer in a mine. When he returned to Seoul, he remarried and came to my grandmother's house to take me back to his new family, but I was nowhere to be found. He stopped by many times, anticipating my return, but he left empty-handed each time. He had no idea how or where to look for me. This time, he received a message from my grandmother shortly after my return, telling him that his son had come back.

But I didn't know any of this at the time. As far as I was concerned, my father had deserted me. I made it clear that I wanted to stay with my grandmother and I didn't want to go with him. He practically dragged me to his home in Youngdeungpo, just south of Seoul. There, a new life awaited me. More food, warmer blankets, a stepmother, and even a grandfather. But rather than feeling privileged, I couldn't ignore the awkwardness of sharing a single room with strangers. I didn't blame my stepmother for feeling uncomfortable either. She had no obligations to take care of me, especially when I caught the measles!

The greatest benefit of staying at my father's house was that out of concern for my education, he registered me at the local elementary school. This short exposure to education helped me apply the things I learned to my life on the streets, and later, studying in America.

I spent that winter trying to make myself invisible to an intimidating father, and an unapproachable stepmother. With the excuse of visiting my grandmother in Geumchon, I left my father's home and returned to the Seoul Train Station.

Whenever life became impossible, I sought the protection of my grandmother, but each time I returned, she greeted me with, "What are you doing here? You belong with your father. You should go to Youngdeungpo." I would stay as long as I could before "going to my father's" but when I left, I just headed straight back to the Seoul Train Station. I wanted to go to school, but I didn't have the courage to impose myself on people I barely knew.

One day my father showed up at my grandmother's while I was taking my "periodic break from street life." This time I followed my father home without much resistance, but found that the circumstances there had changed over the years, and not for the better. The room remained the same, but the family had grown. My stepmother already had more than she could handle with her own children now. She needed help, not another child to take care of.

I decided to lift some of her burden by restaging my disappearance.

"If you need me, I'll be in Geumchon for a few days," and a few hours later I was back on the streets of Seoul. Leaving for a second time was even harder than the first, and my footsteps seemed to falter, but I wanted to help.

forbidden love

In 1945, Japan surrendered to the Allied Forces, ending World War II, and Korea was finally freed from Japanese domination. Even if a beggar's predicament remained the same, for a few months I joined the revelry of an emancipated republic. People walked the streets with eagerness and a new perspective on life.

All the street beggars benefited from the liberation, because now we could spend relaxed nights in the train station, or proudly strut the streets as if we owned the world. We heard that a Korean Police Force had been formed, but controlling communist activities occupied most of their time, and they never bothered to regulate harmless beggars. The privileges of freedom blew a warm breath over that winter, and I welcomed spring with more confidence and dignity.

Liberated or oppressed, however, the threat of winter never

disappeared. One winter flew by in the thrill of independence, but liberation quickly became irrelevant. Winter returned more aggressively than ever, but my threshold for pain had weakened from the lull. My fingers and toes were so numb from frostbite that the torture of imminent paralysis was more terrorizing. Every night I bid the world farewell, only to wake up in the morning and celebrate my success in coming a day closer to spring.

In order to alleviate my starvation one day, I knocked at the front door of a generously large house. A man with an air of ownership opened the door, and instead of slamming the door in my face or commanding one of his workers to throw me some leftovers, he sized me up and down, as I waited anxiously. After a cruel silence, he finally said, "You're a good-looking boy! Why are you out begging?"

"Excuse me?"

"Why is a healthy boy like you knocking on doors and taking scraps from strangers?"

"Uh...I don't know of any other way to survive."

"Why don't you work here? I'll feed you and give you a place to stay."

"Do you really mean that?"

I couldn't believe my sudden change of fortune. I became an employee at Mr. Park's home, along with a servant couple, a male servant, and two cows. We served Mr. Park, his wife, and daughter.

I spent an insecure first night in the servant's room, but by the time I returned from feeding the cows the next morning, I noticed that there was a place for me at the breakfast table. I finished the rice without taking the time to chew, and washed it all down with a bowl of soup. Bursting with excitement, I went back to the barn to earn my food. After a few hours of running some errands, I ate my lunch, found more work, ate dinner, and completed the day working with the cows. As soon as I wrapped myself in the comfortable blankets, I lost the fatigue of the day and all feelings of anxiety or tension escaped. I wondered why I never sought the joy of working to earn my own food and warmth, instead of waiting on the charity of others. Without work, whether I'm living in a home or begging on the streets, I'd be a bum just the same. I felt extremely proud and content.

Spring came. The green meadows and blossoming flowers brought cheerful tunes to my lips because the ability to work was the greatest blessing of all. Bathing the cows felt more like playing in the water, and strolling around in a picture perfect world blinded me from any disappointments.

Every once in a while Mr. Park complimented my hard work, making me believe I was the luckiest guy alive. The other servants treated me like their own brother, and even Mrs. Park started to accept me as a legitimate, hired servant. I had found a family that needed me and appreciated my services. However, I never felt completely at ease around the daughter and avoided her whenever possible.

In my eyes, she was the prettiest girl in town, and she usually stayed in her room studying, but when she needed a break, she quietly joined me in the fields to read, or help me work. True, I feared she might get sun burnt, or worried about the grass staining her dress, but for some reason, I enjoyed her company...and the irregular beating of my heart wasn't such a bad feeling either.

The family started to notice their daughter's frequent disappearances, and frowned upon her reappearing with me. One day she admitted, "My mom won't let me see you anymore. If my mom finds me here, I'll probably get in trouble, but I really don't care."

"It's in your best interest."

"You don't know what it's like to be confined in a room all day. It's really suffocating! And I like being here with you."

I couldn't make her stay home or stay away from me. Her mom eventually found out we had defied her orders, and I took full responsibility for our disobedience.

"Who do you think you are? You don't deserve to have any association with my daughter! I already warned you, now get out! Don't think about coming near our home again!"

Without a chance to explain, I was chased out of the house. Even Mr. Park kept his mouth shut.

"I'm sorry. Wherever you go, try your best, and keep up all your hard work," was the last I heard from anyone in the Parks' household. I left without saying good-bye to the other servants, whom I had grown close to.

As I walked away, I looked back many times, but I never even caught a glimpse of the pretty daughter.

Since tasting the satisfaction of work, I couldn't return to the streets as a beggar. I stayed at the Park's residence long enough to ·

learn the value of hard work. This lesson practically determined my successes, and helped me recover from failures. Since my fortunate encounter with the Parks, I don't recall a period when I ever stopped working. Some may call it the symptoms of a workaholic, but I feel satisfaction when I can claim my rewards are well deserved.

I knocked on the door of what appeared to be the largest home in a neighboring village, and when the door opened I nervously asked, "I was wondering...would you be interested in using me as a servant in your house?"

In times of trouble

After WWII, Korea fell victim to an ideological war called the Cold War. The struggle between communist and non-communist powers came to an agreement along the 38th parallel, dividing Korea in two. A communist government took control of the North, and the South set up a democratic republic.

Foreign powers disregarded domestic cultural boundaries and arbitrarily partitioned the country according to political convenience. It was a temporary accommodation till Koreans could govern autonomously, but people feared a communist invasion and prepared for the worst.

All the rumors and premonitions became a reality. The Korean War exploded on June 25th of 1950. With the support of the former Soviet Union, North Korea invaded South Korea without a declaration of war, to unify "Korea" under communism. The U.N.

general assembly regarded it as an act of invasion and agreed to send armed forces to defend democracy. Twenty-two nations sent troupes to deter the "Korean Conflict".

Without taking time to evaluate the consequences, I took the next train out to my grandmother's home in Geumchon. I worried how they would manage, but more than anything I didn't know if I could ever see her again. While everyone else rushed south, I hurried north.

When I surprised my grandmother that night, instead of welcoming me, she yelled at me for my foolishness.

"You should be running away to the South! Why did you come here? This is too close to the border!"

I slept through the explosions, but early the next morning, my grandmother woke me up, and ordered me to find my father if I wanted to escape the communists.

"I want to stay here. Grandma, no…" I pleaded.

"You must leave now, my child."

"I don't want to go!"

"Do you know what happens if the communists catch you?"

"But Grandma…"

"Don't worry about us. Here, take this."

She handed me a bowl of rice and some red pepper sauce as a meal for my journey. I took the food my grandmother handed me and slipped away before she could see my eyes water.

The loud weapons and the rumbling of the engine started to collide as I looked out the train window to see American jets flying north. Everybody watched anxiously as the jets disappeared. Most people expected the train to halt before reaching the Seoul Station, so when the train stopped at Shinchon, everyone rushed out of the train without a complaint. My stomach kept reminding me of the food my grandmother packed me, but I didn't dare disrupt the current.

Soldiers ordered us to hurry across the bridge, but a mutual understanding already urged our feet to run across with fear.

I searched my memory to find my way to my father's home. Everybody was already preparing to escape the communists when I arrived.

"Uh...I've come to help."

"Hobom?!?"

"I'm so glad you're here!" my grandfather seemed genuinely thrilled, my stepmother seemed shocked to see that I came of my own accord, and my father showed that he really appreciated my willingness to contribute to the family in a time of need.

Shortly after, a loud explosion caught everyone's attention. The Han River Bridge had disappeared. By this time, everyone was frantic to get as far south as possible. If I had hesitated for a couple more hours, I would have lost my chance to cross the bridge...or I could have been a part of the explosion. I still shudder when I consider how the course of my life could have changed with the variation of a few hours.

We packed the necessities and planned to leave as soon as the sun rose. We would start an unknown journey on foot. As we gathered our belongings, my grandfather suddenly refused to go.

"Father..."

"I'll only hold you kids back. I've lived my life, I don't expect much more...and I definitely don't want to be a burden."

"Grandfather, come with us!"

"I can take care of myself. Don't worry about me and just go!"

"Grandfather...I can carry you. Then you won't be slowing us down...and we can all be together!" But that was just wishful thinking. My father carried a load of blankets and my stepmother carried one of the younger children on her back as she balanced another load on her head. I had enough responsibilities of my own. At fifteen years-old, fulfilling my duties as the eldest wasn't easy. I also carried a younger sibling on my back, and filled my hands with more baggage.

I gave my grandfather the untouched meal I brought from my grandmother's and tried to convince myself we would meet again.

Further and further south we moved, but the lack of a specific destination made an exhausting journey increasingly impossible. However, the comfort of family subdued my despair, and strengthened my conviction. I belonged with them, and I was playing a vital role in the journey.

By the time we reached Suwon, a city approximately 20 miles south of Seoul, people had already abandoned their homes, allowing us to feast on the forgotten food. Thanks to the war, all lines of possession blurred, and no one found time to argue the rights of ownership.

The next day, we moved to Pyeongtaek, but unlike the previous night, the houses overflowed with refugees. We found a small corner in the chicken coop to spend the night. I didn't feel too much discomfort with the arrangement, but for a family unaccustomed to a homeless life, an unbearable night of crying, complaining, and trying to adjust, ended in a shivering panic. Because of the early morning dew, we waited for the sun to continue our journey.

At the Pyeongtaek River we were faced with the dead bodies floating downstream. I turned away in disgust, but turned back for a second glance because the dead bodies felt no different from a tree log or branch. I realized how hollow bodies became when detached from the soul.

UN soldiers came to set up a defense barricade to prevent the Communists from penetrating further south.

That night, the screams of women echoed through the night. The soldiers could not resist physical desires and took advantage of the young women. Elders of the town could only murmur their disapproval.

"Whose side are they on anyways?"

"We won't have a single virgin left after feeding their appetites."

It seemed that Koreans could not avoid the attack coming from all directions.

A family struggling to stay together could not compete with the speed of a trained army. Communists eventually raided the city of Pyeongtaek, and even pursued ahead of us. We found no reason to follow them, so we shifted our direction west, to reach the village of Sucheon, South Chungcheong Province. The peaceful village seemed oblivious to the commotion and chaos dictating the rest of the nation.

We claimed an empty house, and unpacked our things. My parents joined the village farm work right away, while I stood guard within the home. Wherever we went, however, we could not avoid the Communists for long. Once they captured an area, not only were we indoctrinated with Communist teachings and anthem, we were forced to witness the morbid executions of any villager showing opposition. They wanted to strictly enforce their authority. Everyone tiptoed around, afraid of attracting attention.

Having been cornered by the Communists again, my father realized that they were not going to stop until they infiltrated every single village in the southern peninsula, so he decided to lead the family back to Youngdeungpo. The greatest factor influencing his decision, I believe, was the thought of my grandfather facing the torture alone.

As the oldest, I took care of my responsibilities of watching over my siblings, and providing food for a hungry family. I conveniently referred to my independent life style, and found that accommodating a larger family fed me with motivation.

We all returned anxiously to see the condition of my grandfather. He was lucky to be alive, but his debilitated health was evident. He passed away a few months later, but before he died, he made me promise him that I would prosper and lead a successful life.

the shining house boy

On my 15th birthday, the United Nations Forces, led by General Douglas Macarthur, made an amphibious landing in Incheon, forcing the communist troops out of Seoul, back across the 38th parallel. As they retreated, they sent all the large buildings in the capital city up in flames. Across the Han River, a sea of fire seemed to foreshadow the apocalypse, and gave me a glimpse of hell.

The U.S. Army Corps of engineers built a temporary bridge on the Han River to transport troops into Seoul and beyond. An endless procession of army trucks containing the foreigners stirred excitement throughout the villages, and gathered crowds pushing to get a closer look at the "big-nosed" soldiers. I welcomed the distraction, and joined the audience.

Shy soldiers smiled, or ignored their spectators, while the extroverts waved as if they had just won a beauty pageant. The generous soldiers threw out chocolate, gum, and other snacks to the children.

"Hello! Hello! Candy! Gum! Give me candy! Give me gum!"

This became a universal chant for children begging the soldiers for sweets all across the nation. If someone lucked out and caught something, they immediately ripped off the wrapping, and swallowed it whole whether it was chocolate, candy, or gum.

With nothing else to do, I went to the bridge every day to holler for gum and candy, but I never really stood out in the crowd. One day, a soldier extended his hand towards me. I reached out expecting to receive a handful of sweets, but instead, he gripped my hand and pulled me into the truck.

As I looked around at the other soldiers, I felt a temporary rush of excitement that vanished as soon as the truck started to move. Panic set in, and the foreign language aggravated my fear. One of the soldiers must have sensed my intention to jump, because he gave me a piece of chocolate. "What could this be?" Soft, sweet, and even slightly bitter!

Next, they tried me with a piece of gum. All the soldiers watched me with amusement, and motioned for me to keep chewing. "What kind of magic candy is this?" I thought. It did not melt or dissolve no matter how hard I chewed. I was completely absorbed in this new discovery, when one of the soldiers came near and sprayed a mist on me. I initially thought the bottle contained some sort of poison, but I started to smell the cologne competing with my foul body odor.

Later I learned that my selection from the crowd wasn't just a random stroke of luck. My grimy face and clothes assured the soldiers that I had nowhere to call home, and no family looking or waiting for me. Perhaps that's why I never struggled to get out of the truck either.

Our truck stopped at the army headquarters in Yongsan, a few miles north of the Han River. It was a former rice patty, cleared out and leveled for an ocean of tents.

The soldiers took off my filthy clothes, put me through an extensive sanitation process, and gave me an army uniform to wear. I had to fold up the sleeves and legs so they didn't drag on the floor or cover my hands. Before I had a chance to fully appreciate my new outfit, someone walked in with combat boots...for me. In retrospect, those army boots must have imposed enormous weight and discomfort for someone unaccustomed to wearing any shoes. But as far as I was concerned, those boots felt like wings as I walked, jumped, and danced around just to feel them on my feet. Bathed in hot water, a fresh hair cut, new clothes, and now even boots! I felt like a beggar waking up to find himself living a dream.

It must have been mealtime, because they took me to a large hall, and gave me a tray with a piece of potato, some beans, and a large piece of meat. I ate the potato and beans, but I didn't want to waste the valuable meat in a single meal, so I wrapped it in a piece of napkin, put it in my pocket, and savored it piece by piece, until the next meal, when I received another piece of meat. I decided not to inconvenience myself with the unnecessary effort again.

That night, I had but one concern: "What if someone steals my boots while I'm sleeping?" I tried falling asleep with them on, but I found that impossible, so I held them close, like a little girl cuddling her favorite stuffed animal, and fell asleep.

I experienced the most comfortable two weeks of my life. The soldiers tested me with simple chores and errands. At the end of two weeks, they reassigned me to the 84th Combat Engineer/Construction Battalion, where the serious labor awaited. The 84th Battalion was located about thirty miles north of Seoul, directly near the battle grounds, which meant greater exposure to danger.

I was selected to work as a houseboy for the officers residing at the top of a hill. There was one tent for the battalion commander, two more for the rest of the officers, and one mess hall.

My days started at five a.m., carrying five gallons of fuel up the hill to start a fire. The officers were asleep, so I tried to keep as silent as possible.

"Who is it?" A light sleeper had already heard my footsteps on my first day at work, and demanded I reveal my identity.

"Goo-duh mo-ning-guh sah!" (Good morning, Sir!)

"What?"

"Goo-duh mo-ning-guh sah!!"

"What did you say?"

"GOO-DUH MO-NING-GUH SAH!!!"

"I can't understand a damn word you're saying."

My voice grew increasingly louder as I repeated my morning greeting, but no one understood my thick accent. In the meantime, I woke up everyone in the surrounding tents.

The house boy at his chores:
A house boy's demands require diligence and muscles.
Carrying oil containers up the stairs first thing in the morning was a better work out than anything I could find in a gym.

Once I placed water over the fire, I polished boots and straightened out their clothes. At seven o'clock, I rushed out to the officers' mess hall to help with chores around the kitchen and prepare breakfast. All the Koreans gathered around to eat rice once we finished serving the meals. Laundry, cleaning, ironing...I had plenty to do, and before I knew it, I returned to the kitchen to help prepare dinner. My days ended around nine p.m., and I was free to sleep, or do whatever I wanted.

The officers appreciated my obedience, and nicknamed me "Buckshot" for the speed and accuracy of my work. I wondered how the soldier pulled me out of a huge crowd of "dirty, lookalikes", but I was eternally grateful for the selection. I compare his hand to a Savior's hand, delivering me from the streets, and introducing a whole new purpose to my life. I really wish I could find him somehow to genuinely thank him for delivering me from a life of erratic change, into a life with direction.

I was most amazed to hear that I would be paid for my services. After invalidating my daily concerns of "Where should I sleep? What should I eat? They wanted to compensate me? How absurd!" If they wished to pay me, however, I had no objections.

As I adjusted to my work, I started to observe minor details, and became more aware of my environment.

In the tents for the non-commissioned, enlisted men, beds and cigarette smoke occupied the whole room, leaving no personal space, or an atmosphere to rest. Their meals tasted almost indigestible, and the laundry facilities, far from satisfactory.

The officers, however, enjoyed spacious living conditions; their clothes washed, even ironed daily; and they ate very well-balanced, nutritious meals.

I saw personality disparities determine how soldiers controlled their emotions in unforeseen circumstances. The different approaches to life went beyond hierarchy or rank in the battalion. The talkative versus the quiet, the extroverts and introverts, selfish and considerate, greedy and generous, the list goes on. In their spare time, some drank, smoked, played cards and gambled, while others read books, even practiced musical instruments. The variety of characters also affected how each soldier faced their own destiny, especially death. Some screamed, yelled, blamed people, while others silently shook with fear, cried, or prayed.

Even as builders and repairmen of roads and bridges on the front, the risk of injury remained high. When a soldier left in the morning, no one could predict whether he would return walking, carried on a stretcher, or wrapped in a body bag. Some came back without an arm, others without a leg. Many did not return at all. I watched a soldier mourn his amputated legs, and bid his dream to become a basketball star farewell. Someone could grieve a friend's death today, but pick a meaningless fight with another friend tomorrow. I always wondered why these soldiers came to such a poverty stricken country to sacrifice their own blood for nominal compensation. I especially admired those who visited orphanages with treats for the children.

Even when explosions echoed through the camp, soldiers sat in front of a large screen, watching famous movie stars profess their love to each other. Unable to join the soldiers, houseboys sat on a hill overlooking the screen, to share the emotional manipulation of a movie. Elizabeth Taylor could steal the hearts of every man present, within a matter of minutes.

Of the six officers I served, James Booth, an African-American Lieutenant, stood out because of his skin color. Some avoided him, and others deliberately left him out of social gatherings. I kept a comfortable distance too.

One night, I found him crying by himself. Surprised and feeling a bit awkward, I turned to walk away, but he called my name. Even as I sat in front of him, he continued to cry, so I asked why he was crying. He showed me his hands and replied in frustration, "It's because of my color. Because I'm black." He took his hands and started to bite into them as if removing his hands would eliminate his problem. I set my own hand on his, to show my sympathy, and cried with him to share his pain. I finally realized why he remained a Lieutenant, long after he should have been promoted to a Captain. From then on I kept his shoes shining brighter, ironed his uniform neater, made his bed tighter, and gave him a smile of encouragement whenever I saw him.

Then there was Captain Maraska, who put the end of a Carvin in his mouth, pulled the trigger with his toes, and blew away his life. He always made many mistakes in his work because he was rarely sober. But learning that his wife had taken his three children to live with another man destroyed his will to live, and activated his suicidal inclination.

Soldiers covered his body with a large plastic bag, and threw it into a truck that drove away like it contained unnecessary cargo. I found Captain Maraska's glasses near his bloodstain, so I preserved it for a while as if it held a remnant of the captain's soul.

On a warm, sunny day, Sergeant Hanson took me to a place, and gave me a whistle. He needed me to stand watch while he took care of some business, and ordered me to blow the whistle as soon as I spotted an MP (military police) jeep approaching. The sudden appearance of an MP jeep startled my nerves and impaired my coordination. To see the MP dragging out a naked Sergeant and a woman equally exposed surprised me even more. Due to dangers of sexually transmitted diseases and for the protection of civilians, army regulations strictly prohibited any association with prostitutes. The MP made surprise appearances at whorehouses to enforce these laws.

The next time I saw Sergeant Hanson, he had been demoted to a private. I avoided him with fear of punishment, even if a part of me wanted to get it over with, but he acted as if nothing happened, and dismissed the whole incident.

I spent my pubescent years in the barracks, surrounded by sexually frustrated men. With no one to talk to, and lack of attention, I suffered through mood swings alone, and cried myself to sleep on countless occasions. Sometimes, I imagined my happiest moments, and relived them in my mind. I even tried to wash away my emotions with alcohol, but I quickly learned that in the morning, an unpleasant feeling replaced the temporary elation of the previous night.

I discovered a cure for my depression. When I received my paycheck, I bought a bagful of treats, and passed them out at nearby orphanages. I felt like Old St. Nick himself.

The joy in the children's faces brought me contentment, and above all, I enjoyed hearing the harmony of a roomful of children chewing gum. During naptime, chewed gum decorated the walls, but when the children awoke, the gum disappeared from the walls, returned to their mouths, and the harmony resumed.

I started to realize the power of money. If someone had taught me the value of money in advance, I would have set aside some money for savings, but ignorance comes with consequences.

In some emergency cases, I elevated to the position of an official interpreter, and helped Colonel O'Grady, the battalion commander, with my severely broken English.

Growing up amidst the insecurities of life and death, exposure to racial prejudices and social hierarchy could hardly be considered a privilege. However, when I grabbed the soldier's hand, it meant more than a free ride in an army truck. It was God's way of reaching out to me. I turned my back on a futile existence, and faced a constructive life.

Youth preserved amidst war and uncertainty...
Life and death confused just across the field,
and greater uncertainties awaiting beyond the mountains,
but blue skies preserve the innocence in the fields and my youth
remains hopeful.

encounter

Alcohol and gambling consoled the apprehensive soldiers, and occupied most of their free time. Those who valued nothing more than their own lives expressed their frustration through their actions, and in their language.

Captain Ray Paull, the army dentist, intrigued my curiosity with his pious and gentle ways, but he earned my respect as a scholar and a moral leader. His withdrawn and angelic personality inspired most, but others accused him for being arrogant and self-righteous.

When I earned my first paycheck, I felt the need to show my appreciation by treating the officers to some authentic Korean fruits. I went to the market and purchased a variety of fruits costing over half of my monthly paycheck. I presented a nice array of Korean fruits before them, but unfamiliar with the exotic fruits, and skeptical of the sanitation of Korean produce, nobody initiated the taste test. Noticing the awkward situation, Captain Paull reached out with a smile, and gratefully accepted my treat. Only then did the others begin to enjoy the fruit.

I frequently listened to the sound of Captain Paull's organ music flowing out of the tent chapel. Listening to the soothing sound reminded me of my own miseries, and I would cry out with self-pity to console myself. On one particular night, I felt so overwhelmed with loneliness and grief that I couldn't control my sobs. I had been crying for some time when I sensed a long shadow blocking the moonlight. I looked up to find Captain Paull standing before me.

"Go away!" I shouted, ashamed and embarrassed for allowing an American officer to see me in an emotional breakdown.

"Buckshot, why are you crying?"

"It's none of your business! I want you to leave me alone!"

"I have three sons at home. It hurts me to see my children cry, and I want to know why you are crying."

He handed me a neatly folded handkerchief to wipe my tears, but I started to cry even harder. His compassion mitigated my sorrow, and allowed me to open up a little.

"I feel so lonely."

"Where's your family?"

"I don't know."

Too late to take back his inappropriate question, he squeezed my arms and gave me a hug so gentle, yet affirming. I had never felt so close to anyone before, but the most surprising fact was that it felt strangely comforting. His embrace generated a sense of hope and love that I never knew existed. The source and the effect of love were both foreign, and hard for me to accept at the time, but since then, I return to the moment he opened his arms to me every time I feel lonely or discouraged. When I came to know Christ, God's unconditional love was easy for me to accept because I understood His love through the love Captain Paull displayed for me—a love that extends to the most insignificant beings, a love great enough to cover all my scars, and a love I desired. I still remember the comfort of his warmth, and aspire to share the same kind of reassurance with others.

In fear of ruining his mood with my depression, I wiped my tears and stood up. He walked me all the way back to my tent. Before I walked inside, he looked down at me and said, "I'll pray that God takes away your pain."

I had never heard about God in that context before, so I assumed that God must be someone in America.

"What is 'pray'?"

"I'll tell you some other time. It's late. Go in and get some rest."

The next day, Captain Paull found me working in the kitchen and handed me a small Bible. My pride refused to admit that I didn't know how to read English, so I just accepted the gift.

A few days later, he asked me to meet him in front of the main gate of the battalion after work. By the time I got there, he was already waiting for me with a truck full of lumber. Disappointment replaced my respect for the captain when I thought he was going to use the lumber to make profit in the black market. The place he took me was not a black market, but a site to build a refugee camp for those fleeing communism. I eagerly helped in every way possible.

We built a small temporary clinic with a wooden table, a couple chairs and a makeshift roof, and I became his interpreter for the patients who came to the clinic. Captain Paull inspired me to make an attempt to read the Bible he gave me, so I bribed an interpreter in the Korean battalion to teach me how to read English, starting with the alphabet. Learning to read was much more difficult than I expected, and just because I could pronounce a word didn't mean I understood it, so I bought myself an English-Korean dictionary.

As I started to feel more comfortable around Captain Paull, I worked up the courage to ask for an explanation about his moral and spiritual manner.

"Why are you so different from the rest of the soldiers?"

"I don't know what you mean...maybe it's because I believe in God. Even in the battle field, His presence protects me and gives me reassurance."

"Who's God?"

"You really don't know?"

"Does he live in America?"

"What?"

"Is he a friend of yours in America?"

Realizing how little I knew about religion, he started to laugh.

My father of hope, Ray Paull
Our encounter epitomized hope.
How capable are we of loving our neighbors as ourselves?
Ray Paull extended an invitation to me as his son,
loved me as his son,
and unlocked a future for me that would not have
been possible without love.

"God is the One Who created this world. He created you and me. He is my Father, and He's also your Father. My sons are God's children just like you."

I couldn't even begin to comprehend his religious beliefs, and just muttered under my breath, "But I thought Kwangsung Shin was my father."

"Then does God even love people like me?"

"Of course. God loved us so much that He sent Jesus Christ, as our Savior to die for our sins, and whoever believes this will receive everlasting life."

"Then is Jesus Christ an American?"

Again, I assumed that he must be a friend in America.

Growing closer to Captain Paull stimulated my curiosity, and I wanted to meet this God that made him so different. The more time I spent with him, the more I wanted to be like him. His warm smile, kind heart, his willingness to serve...if he received all the qualities from God...if he could share some of his peace, and give me hope for the future...give me comfort...

i trust You

Lunchtime had come and gone many hours ago by the time I returned to the base after helping out on the frontline as a temporary interpreter for the battalion commander. I went into the kitchen hoping to find something to eat, but Corporal Castle, the cook in the officer's mess hall, refused to let me have any food outside of designated meal hours. When I tried to find food for myself, he picked up a knife, pushed it against my throat, and threatened to kill me if I didn't leave immediately.

In a sudden impulse to defend myself, I threw his weight over my shoulder and watched him fall hard on his back while the knife slipped from his hands. Shocked and humiliated, Corporal Castle dashed out of the kitchen and reported the incident to the first sergeant, except he claimed that I tried to kill him, instead of admitting that he attacked me first. The military police stormed in to arrest me. Their sudden appearance made me forget the little English I knew, so nobody spoke in my defense.

The other Americans only knew that I attempted to kill their fellow soldier, so they all yelled, "Kill! Kill!" as they took turns kicking, punching, spitting, and throwing insults at me.

"Just wait till the battalion commander returns. You'll be sorry for what you did! How dare a Gook like you attack an American soldier?"

I waited in the first sergeant's office, unaware of Corporal Castle's claims, and wondered what I did to deserve the arrest. I was always aware of my subordinate status, but at the time, I felt more vulnerable than a bug.

About two hours later, the doors flew open, and a stunned Captain Paull rushed in.

"Tell me what happened, Buckshot! Did you really try to kill Castle? I just need to hear 'yes' or 'no'."

"No Sir!"

"Buckshot, I trust you."

With that, Captain Paull left the room. Shortly after, the military police returned, untied my hands and told me to go and help prepare dinner. Corporal Castle ignored me while we worked, and I was serving the tables when Captain Paull called Corporal Castle out to the mess hall. The captain forced Castle's hand on a bible, and made him take an oath before God, and everyone present.

"Did Buckshot really try to kill you?"

The only way for Castle to avoid the question was to keep silent.

"Answer me!"

Castle still kept his mouth shut.

In a more threatening voice, Captain Paull said, "Let me ask you the question again. Did Buckshot try to kill you? Say 'yes' or 'no'."

The tension in that room almost snapped as everyone held their breath. After a few excruciatingly long seconds of silence, Castle shouted, "No Sir!" and ran into the kitchen.

Everyone resumed breathing, and I felt a relief wash over me. Captain Paull spoke out, "I never doubted Buckshot's innocence. He could not have attempted to kill Corporal Castle."

Castle's testimony cleared my name, and the other officers stepped up to apologize. As soon as I knew my precarious situation had been resolved, all the tears that I had been holding in since the accusations all poured out.

After that incident, my gratitude and reverence for Captain Paull exceeded limits or boundaries. He must have compromised his own position by defending me over the American soldier. I began to feel the joy of building a trust with someone who cared about me. Working with him in the refugee clinic rose to a higher level of satisfaction, and I discovered the fruitfulness of sharing the little I had to offer.

Captain Paull stood against his own to defend an inferior. His courage and faith proved my innocence. Our relationship dissolved all racial, language, and age barriers, and even progressed with the triumph of my traumatizing experience.

One evening, in the jeep returning from the refugee clinic, he carefully asked me, "Would you like to become my son?"

"What?" I thought I misunderstood the question.

"I want to adopt you and bring you to America with me. I've already spoken with the rest of my family in America. Now it's up to you to decide."

I started to remember the subtle hints he had been placing throughout the months. I had been worrying about what I would do when Captain Paull returned to America, but I never imagined joining him.

Without a doubt in my mind, I accepted his invitation, and vowed to myself, "I will follow this man to the ends of the earth, even to the depths of hell."

following a rainbow

The stench of blood seeped through the earth from the battlefields just over the mountain. Even when the houseboys spent days cutting and watering the grass, planting and taking care of flowers, death constantly threatened the lives of those around us.

I welcomed summer because it eliminated the tedious chores of carrying heavy fuel for building fires, or heating water over the fire, but I especially treasured the longer days I spent with Captain Paull. I helped at the refugee camps, and tried to emulate his benevolent heart.

Captain Paull didn't drink alcohol, but he really enjoyed ice-cold water, which was hard to come across in the heat of summer. I discovered the battalion commander's icebox, and took advantage of an empty whiskey bottle. I washed it, filled it with water, and secretly chilled it with the other beverages in Colonel

O'Grady's icebox.

One day, Colonel O'Grady caught me taking the bottle from his icebox and accused me of stealing from him. I tried to explain that the bottle contained water for Captain Paull and not whiskey, but he dismissed my justification.

"This icebox belongs to me and not Ray Paull. I don't ever want to see you near it again!"

My greatest regret was that I could no longer have the pleasure of preparing the ice-cold water for the captain, and watch his satisfaction after quenching his thirst.

At the end of two sleepless nights of reviewing alternatives, I found a solution. I spent another two days digging a hole about five feet deep, and put in a round metal sheet to prevent the walls from caving in. It wouldn't be as cold as the icebox, but I hoped that the depth of the soil would retain the temperature. Captain Paull might have wondered why I failed to provide for him his daily glass of "ice water" for the few days, but as soon as I dug my hole and made sure my hypothesis worked, I resumed my responsibility. Until another officer told Captain Paull how I prepared the cold water, he had no idea that cold water could be so scarce. When he heard this, Captain Paull came to me and gave me the warmest hug because he didn't know how else to thank me.

A few days later, he presented a whole new outfit for me. He had to order it from Sears & Roebuck in America, because it was unavailable in Korea. Our feeling was mutual. We would go to great lengths to show our love for each other.

Towards the end of summer, in order to process my adoption

application, Captain Paull took me to Busan, the second largest city in Korea, located on the southeastern tip of the country, in which the temporary South Korean government existed. I always ran the risk of being forced into the Korean army, so Captain Paull put me on a plane while he took the train.

I had never ridden a plane before...the thought never even crossed my mind. I was going to fly higher and faster than the birds. I buckled my seat belt feeling secure and excited, while the plane started rolling away from the gate. Once the plane established the speed and force to lift off, my world started to change. My stomach churned, my head pounded, and worst of all, my ears were screaming. The stewardess recognized my bewilderment as the familiar symptoms of someone's first exposure to aviation. She advised me to plug my nose, blow hard, and then swallow. I followed her instruction to find that the strange feelings diminished, but I was so embarrassed. Now I just needed to find a way to hide under my seat.

By the time I reached the Busan airport, Captain Paull was waiting for me with a jeep. It took three days to complete the necessary paper work, and those three days provided a series of obstacles. We asked around to find the Ministry of Foreign Affairs, Internal Affairs, and the Ministry of Justice, but no one knew exact locations, and everyone told us a different version.

Under the heat of the sun, we wished for rain to settle the excessive dust, but when the rain began to pour, we waited for the sun to dry our clothes. After a long day of commotion, we couldn't even anticipate a comfortable night of rest. Whether I slept in a military base or a nearby motel, I snuck in invisibly, and rushed out early in the morning to avoid the curious eyes capable of reporting me to the Korean military service.

Throughout the whole time, not a single word of complaint dared to linger at Captain Paull's lips. I couldn't understand why he would go through so much trouble to keep a promise to an insignificant houseboy. I saw it as a pure example of absolute selflessness, and I wondered if his religion had something to do with it.

"Captain, are you a good person because you're a Christian?"

"Despite my imperfections, I'm trying my best to live a righteous life."

Spending so much time with my object of reverence helped me achieve a clear idea of how I wanted to construct my life, and without my awareness, a spiritual conversion took place.

Captain Paull didn't have much time left in Korea, and he wanted to make sure I was in a safe environment in his absence. He asked Father Yoon, a Korean priest who came to the battalion every Sunday for Catholic Mass, to take me in as a helping hand in the cathedral. The cathedral was a considerable distance away from the battalion, so my service as a houseboy ended with the priest's acceptance. If I had my way, I would have stayed near Captain Paull for as long as possible, but the otherwise gentle captain remained uncompromising and stern.

I folded my career as a houseboy for the American GI's, and moved my headquarters to the Myeongdong Cathedral in Seoul.

Before I left, Lieutenant Booth called me aside to warn me about the misconceptions of America.

"America isn't the heaven people envision. There's no such thing as a sanctuary. You have to be careful."

His simple advice contained layers of caution. I didn't understand the underlying implications then, but throughout the years, I have been given many reasons to look back on the night I comforted Lieutenant Booth for the racial injustice he suffered.

I lived on the third floor of a brick building built for the clergy within the Myeongdong Cathedral. Throughout the week, I swept the floors, kept the place tidy, and took care of simple errands. On Sunday's, I rang the church bell that called the congregation to worship, and from six a.m. till two p.m., I pushed the pedals of a pipe organ. Compared to the responsibilities of a houseboy, I worked minimum hours, and my tasks were relatively easy.

However, living without the company of Captain Paull made each day feel meaningless and idle.

Here, I met two lifelong friends. We were more different than any trio imaginable, but we connected through our individual dreams and our commitment to rising above obstacles to fulfill these aspirations. Each of us had experiences of tragic loss, and we became a source of comfort in times of depression, and a company of rejoicing in times of happiness.

Woonsub Hwang, an employee of the Catholic Journal was two years older than me, and he was also deprived of a formal education. He lost his father at age two, and lived with his widowed mother and two sisters. The whole family depended on the meager salary Woonsub earned from the church. After his father's death, Woonsub's family was so poor that he had to witness his own sister die of starvation, which is why Woonsub dreamed of becoming a rich man to support his mother and remaining sister. Despite their difficult situation, Woonsub's mother took pity on me, and called me to their home to share delicious meals.

Youngdo Lee lost her husband to the war, and came to the Catholic Church as a maid to support her two children. Even as a single mother, she could not forget her dream to become a teacher, so she attended night school at Sookmyung Women's University, Seoul.

If anyone heard our conversations, they would have laughed at our foolishness. However, we fed each other courage, and found hope in our friendship. We understood the narrow prospect of achieving our goals, but we kept each other accountable not to allow our environment limit the possibilities.

Just as we dreamed, Woonsub kept his promise to become a prosperous businessman, while Youngdo earned her degree and became a teacher. I followed my dream to America and we all kept in touch to continue our relationship.

When Woonsub and Youngdo's children grew up, I helped them study in America. Many years later, Youngdo remarried and immigrated to Seattle. While she went to night school in Korea, I tried to help her by contributing a small amount to her studies, but in Seattle, she helped me and supported me like an older sister.

Both Woonsub and Youngdo have passed on, but I will always cherish their friendship and remember that a dream multiplies when shared.

Captain Paull, now my father, visited me on the weekends with an ice cream cone in his hands. The condition of my melted ice cream and his dust covered uniform made me aware of the difficult journey from the battalion to the cathedral, but out of selfishness, or maybe just innocent longing, I waited for him every Saturday. Once his jeep came into sight, I ran straight towards it to spend the extra seconds with him.

Before we knew it, autumn passed by, and January brought the day of Captain Paull's departure to cast another shadow of separation.

I rode with my father back to the army base, and during the trip I promised myself not to cry as a display of my mature masculinity.

"I'll continue the adoption process in America. You have to keep in touch, ok?" and he gave me a piece of paper containing his contact information.

The minute I received the paper, my determination failed and I couldn't stop the tears from flowing. Even Captain Paull had to turn away more abruptly to hide his own tears.

His jeep left me standing alone in a cloud of dust. In my mind I ran after him, begging him to stay, begging him not to leave. But when the dust disappeared I stood by myself to face a painful reality. I felt more alone than ever before. Only my heart continued to cry out in a silent plea.

He showed me a rainbow...but before I could take a firm grasp of this gift, he was returning to America. Soon, I would join his world, and claim my own rainbow.

a fleeting rainbow

Tides of loneliness flooded my empty heart on the long winter nights. Hoping to feel some form of telepathic connection to Captain Paull, I read the Bible he gave me. I spent many nights with the scriptures and a dictionary, but as the nights turned into a year, and as the second year approached, a benevolent invitation on Father Yoon's part became a burden. My nonexistent lease could not be renewed, and I didn't want to force Father Yoon in an awkward position by ignoring my already overstayed welcome.

Without complaints, I turned my back on the glorious sounds of the pipe organ, carrying a small bag with my belongings. It didn't take me very long to realize that I had nowhere else to go. Without much thought, I just got on a bus and headed north. When I reached the Panmunjom—a village on the de facto border between South and North Korea—vicinity, the familiar scene of the battalions greeted me. A temporary excitement shifted to despair as my regression became evident.

I blindly asked the soldiers to use me in any way they needed, and those who recognized my skills welcomed me back as a houseboy for the officers. Working without a single friend helped me focus and direct my full attention to my work, but the strictly routine life crowded out any room or energy for hope.

In July of 1953, the Armistice Treaty established a cease-fire agreement, and an exchange of prisoners directly followed. As the prisoners of war crossed the 38th parallel, I watched soldiers of all ranks throwing off the hats and clothes of the communist uniform, joyfully dancing with absolute freedom. In contrast, the communist prisoners also joined in stripping off the opponents' clothes, but they could not share the same enthusiasm of freedom.

Because I had access to a bus, on weekends I met with Woonsub in the Catholic Church. With the probability of leaving for America in mind, I also visited my biological father. My stepmother went out of her way to accommodate a son who may never return. Instead of resenting my adoption as abandoning my family, my father also tried to help me. He gathered all his savings and bought me a phony high school diploma. If I couldn't go to America through the adoption, then he planned to send me as a foreign exchange student. I really appreciated his effort, but even dogs would laugh at an ignorant beggar going to America as a college student.

I never intended to completely abandon my biological family. It wasn't much, but I offered my earnings to help provide for the rest of the family, and I bought various gifts and sweets for my younger siblings.

Overcome with nostalgia, I decided to visit Geumchon one day. I spent the majority of my journey reminiscing on old times, but anxiety gripped my body as I began to anticipate the possibility of my grandmother's death. My delightful excursion turned into nervous hesitation as I uneasily pushed open the picket fence. Before I opened my mouth to call "Grandma?" a second time, I spotted bare feet running in my direction, and released a long sigh.

"Who ever thought I would see you again in this life time? Your mother would have been so proud to see you like this! Returning successfully! I think I can finally rest in peace!"

For such a secluded village, any man returning in an American GI uniform, with leather boots, and a bagful of presents appeared pretty impressive. Fascinated by my transformation, my grandmother stroked, shook and hit me, to overcome her own disbelief.

I unwrapped the gifts and presented them accordingly: American cigarettes for my grandmother and chocolate for my cousins. I remembered a night when I ran away from home determined to return with enough *yeot* to share with the whole village. Many years later, I finally transferred an irrational childhood dream into reality. Watching my cousins enjoy genuine American *yeot* relieved any grudge I still carried.

After witnessing everyone's well being, I turned my back on my crying grandmother who wondered if we would meet again, and shut my eyes to my own tears. My feet never felt so heavy, and I doubted taking off my boots could make a difference. The physical weight was completely irrelevant to the emotional burden of detachment.

I waited for a passport for two years. In order to receive a passport, I needed clearance from the Department of Defense, but due to internal corruption, I couldn't receive clearance without the support of a bribe. My visa expired twice, and if it expired once more, America would remain a fleeting rainbow of my dreams. I understood the dangers and risks of sending people overseas, especially amidst the chaos of war and its aftermath, but the Department officials would purposely ignore my files until they received a bribe.

One day, a rush of optimism directed me to visit the Department of Defense office.

"You're here again?" a major greeted me.

The excitement from his recognition blinded me from the possibility of ulterior motives, and I readily obeyed when he motioned for me to follow him. I thought he wanted to help me, so I followed him to a Chinese restaurant. The major ordered all sorts of delicious foods from the menu, and without extending an invitation he finished all the food alone. He rinsed his mouth with water, let out a long, tasty burp, and patted my back saying, "Thanks for lunch. Take care of the bill. See you in a bit." That day, I emptied my pockets and scraped out all the lint, but I didn't have enough money to cover the meal. So I used my coat as collateral, and paid the difference by washing dishes for the next few days.

"Are you really going to America?"

"What will you do if you can't go?"

I didn't even want to hear the questions, and I definitely didn't have answers to them.

One day, I received a letter from Captain Paull.

"Buckshot, I have been thinking about your situation for some time. Do you really want to come to America? I don't understand why it should take so long. If you'd rather stay in Korea, I understand. Don't feel obligated to accept my invitation."

My father misunderstood my inability to go, as a reluctance to live in America. I realized I was hiding a dilemma that needed to be exposed. I wrote a letter explaining the circumstances delaying my departure for America. One day, two black jeeps drove up to the battalion. I found no reason to pay particular attention to their arrival, until I heard a man say, "We are here to look for Mr. Hobom Shin." My instincts commanded me to run away, but my identity had already been revealed, and I didn't stand a chance of escape. To my confusion, however, they treated me with utmost respect, and politely helped me into the jeep. They escorted me through the Ministry of Foreign Affairs, the American Embassy, and the Department of Defense to help me receive a passport.

Later, I learned that upon Captain Paull's request, a Senator in his Congressional District, Senator Watkins, called the American Ambassador for a favor, and immediately processed my visa. To realize I wasted two years in disappointment and agony because of a simple defect, easily repaired by a phone call, magnified my frustration.

I contacted my father in America.

"Father, I've received my passport."

"Congratulations, Son! I'll send you a plane ticket right away. Hope to see you soon!"

I hung up the phone, turned around, and exploded into tears.

Shortly after, I received an envelope from America containing a plane ticket to Japan, and a ship ticket from Japan to America.

i Kiss you good-bye

September 3, 1955, I finally held the tickets to a new world in my hands. My father sent me a boat ticket to America, via Japan, but in America, they were unaware of the strained relations between Korea and Japan. Travel to Japan was prohibited for Korean citizens, and therefore, I would not be allowed to leave the airport in Japan. If I waited for the animosity between Korea and Japan to subside, my visa would have already expired.

I frantically asked around, and found a solution. A supply ship for the U.S. army was leaving the Busan harbor and sailing directly to America. However, a problem remained. After returning my tickets, I was only ninety-three dollars short, but still an amount I couldn't handle. I had a week till my visa expired for the last time. There wasn't enough time for my father to help me from America, so I didn't even bother sending him a letter. Hopeless and desperate, I sold anything of value that I owned, which amounted to only seven dollars. Where do I find eighty-six dollars?

Despair turned to self-pity, and I returned to all the years of disappointment. "I'm a worthless being...even my biological father abandoned me...how could I be such a fool, relying on an invisible God?"

I reached a point where I wanted to forget about everything and accept my own fate, but when I remembered my father in America, I rebuked myself for my pessimism.

Sunday, September 10, I wandered aimlessly with a burdened heart, and found myself at the steps of the United States 8th Army Chapel. A few of the ushers recognized me as the adopted son of Captain Ray Paull, and asked me when I was leaving for America.

Before I could reply, my head dropped, and tears poured from my eyes.

"What's wrong? What happened?" one of the ushers asked me.

"I don't think I can go to America."

"Why not?"

I reluctantly explained my situation, and shortly after, the Branch Leader stood before the congregation and announced, "Our brother, Dr. Paull has adopted this young man, but he cannot go to America because he is $90 short in purchasing a ticket from Korea to the United States. I'd like to dedicate this time for a special love offering to help our brother in his time of need."

He sent around his hat, and easily collected $230. They gave me $110, and wished me the best of luck.

The departure time for the ship was at eleven a.m. the next day. I rushed to buy my ticket aboard the U.S.S. Contest, and went to Youngdeungpo to gather what was left of my belongings. After saying quick goodbyes, I reached the Seoul Train Station with two hours to spare. I breathed a sigh of relief, and looked around my street life shelter. I used to pick the lice off my clothes on a nearby hill, survived cold winters with nothing but the rags on my back and a worn out blanket if I was lucky. So many sleepless nights, and starving days...

I wanted to erase the shame, indignity and the existence of my previous life style with my departure from Korea. Even when I felt the train running against the tracks, I started to doubt myself again. Can I really get on that ship? What if I miss it? I don't even have money to return to Seoul. Should I return to the streets and beg? As I looked out into the night, images of my friends and family appeared before me. My grandmother, Father, Stepmother, my half-brothers and sister, all my street friends...and finally, Jaewon...

I could draw a map of every alley in Seoul, but now I was leaving my comfort zone, and surrendering my future to the unknown. I embarked on a precarious journey, already too deeply engaged to hesitate. Even with the legitimate seat, I felt like a stowaway in danger of being thrown out of the train.

The sun rose as I arrived in Busan.

Only after I saw the row of ships docked at the harbor did I allow acceptance to replace my uncertainty. I observed the surroundings of the U.S.S. Contest in a cloud of anxiety. About eight others prepared to board the ship. They held flowers and were surrounded by friends and family, but I spent my final moments in Korea alone. Even the wind seemed eager to blow me off the shores. Other families stood near each other to flaunt their wealth, but I segregated myself and moved into isolation. What was the emptiness I still felt even as I stepped into my dreams? I couldn't fully enjoy my excitement for America because of the lurking sense of desertion, combined with the bitterness of my lack of support.

As I climbed up the ship, my legs grew weak beneath me, so I quickly grabbed the rails to control my balance. I entered the ship, followed a sailor to my assigned room, and found a roommate waiting for me. I guess he couldn't judge my social status by my appearance, because after introducing himself, he continued to ask questions irrelevant to someone of my class. Just because he graduated from Seoul National University, and was on his way to Cornell University to further his education, he assumed I was preparing to attend some sort of university as well.

I joined the others on deck to watch the ship pull away from the harbor.

"When will I ever get the chance to return to this land...? But I have no reason to return to a land that caused me so much pain and suffering: a land of social discrimination and inequality, a land of hunger and deprivation."

The least I could do to protect myself was to abandon the

country all together. To me, Korea was not only a victim of oppression, but also the perpetrator.

The ship pulled away from the harbor till only the beauty and splendor of the landscape remained in my sight. Without the garbage in the streets and the anxieties of the people, Korea was a land just as desirable as any other. However, the distance could not transform the image in my mind, and I turned my back in disgust.

I vowed to myself, "I'll never return to this place." As a symbol of my pledge, I leaned over to spit out into the sea.

It gave me some satisfaction, so I spit again and said, "Just as you have forsaken me, I disown you," and spit into the sea one last time.

In Search of a Dream

a new land, a new horizon

As Korea disappeared beyond the horizon, I started to realize that I was headed for a completely different world. The U.S.S. Contest held about 10 crewmembers, a captain, 8 Korean passengers, and me. It was a refrigerated vessel chartered by the U.S. government to carry supplies to the American troops in Korea. Only about 200 feet in length, this tiny cargo ship seemed bigger than the Titanic to me.

When I walked into the dining room of the ship, an American sailor served me my food. I was so unaccustomed to this change of status that I blushed as I accepted it. Who would have thought that I could ever be served?

As we sailed across the Pacific Ocean, our ship felt like a single leaf struggling to stay afloat. Sometimes the waves crashed against the small window in my cabin, and the pressure seemed to threaten my existence. I doubted our ability to reach America, but knowing that the God of Ray Paull created the ocean gave me just enough reassurance to hold my breath.

The other passengers gathered around to share past experiences and future plans, but they were all older than me, and we had nothing in common. Studying abroad is a privilege even today, but at the time, to just consider the possibility required considerable wealth and affluence. I preferred to spend my time with one of the sailors who happened to be from the Philippines. We shared a silent relationship, because neither of us spoke much English.

During meals, everyone fought for a seat next to the captain, but feeling inferior, I eliminated myself from the competition. I still wonder where those men are now…what could they be doing? With so much ambition and power, they must have succeeded immensely. Why else would they be willing to spend so much money on their education?

For fifteen consecutive days, I saw nothing but the ocean and the sky above it. When the captain announced our expected arrival time, everyone, including the sailors, cheered with relief.

The Seattle harbor looked like a vision from a fantasy rather than an inhabited, man-made city. As soon as the ship arrived, everyone was eager to step on solid ground and tour as much of Seattle before returning to leave for San Francisco. After sending my father a telegram to inform him of my arrival, I had less than four dollars in my pocket. I considered staying on the ship, but I decided to follow the rest of the Koreans, and just refrain from spending any money.

The sense of stability I felt from the firm ground beneath my feet brought a deep sigh of relief throughout my whole body.

Not a trace of garbage, not even a single particle of dust covered the asphalt streets. I paid for my lunch, aware of the fact that I only had two dollars remaining. I chose to wash down the meal with my own saliva instead of buying a drink.

As the ship set sail towards San Francisco, I began to panic in my own excitement and terror. Up till now, I could rely on the protection of the ship, but when I step off, who do I trust and depend on? Leaving Korea and adjusting to life on the ship felt like such a big step that I didn't know if I could handle another transition.

Once our ship sailed into the San Francisco Bay, all thoughts disappeared from my mind. I had heard of the magnificence of the bay, but the visual encounter was indescribable. Enchanted by the Golden Gate Bridge, the buildings, and all the surroundings, I had to pinch myself to make sure I wasn't about to wake up from a dream.

When I got off the ship, a Caucasian couple walked towards me and asked, "Are you Buckshot?" They extended their hands to congratulate my arrival. I'd never even seen an American woman in real life...and to shake hands with one! She continued to introduce herself as my Aunt Polly (mother's sister), and her husband Norman. It took me a while to overcome my initial shock, but absorbing the realization that the rest of my family would look more like her than me, sent me into relapse.

At the time, my aunt's home set on a hill just beyond the Golden Gate Bridge looked like a mansion, and the interior made me feel like royalty. When they told me to keep my shoes on, I refused to violate the spotless carpet with dirt from the streets, so I insisted on observing the Korean custom of taking shoes off when indoors. The children returned from school to find the stranger in their home. After quick introductions, we carefully studied each other. As much as I was a foreigner to them, they were intriguing figures to me.

I admired the neat bathrooms, and fancy plates, but the slices of bread jumping out of a toaster brought long forgotten laughter to me.

After dinner, we drove to a hill overlooking the San Francisco skyline. A new horizon welcomed my arrival, and promised me endless possibilities. In a corner of my heart, I questioned God for favoring one nation over another, but more than anything, I thanked Him for leading me to this privileged land.

oNe, twO, thrEe...

One, two, three...
An eternity of stars I see.
Stars celebrating up on high,
Pouring out of the endless sky.

Big star, Little star,
Who holds them in place?
Which one consoles my heart,
In a compassionate embrace?

Twinkle, twinkle, twinkle...

Bright, shimmering lights draw near,
To meet this crystal tear.
The power of reflection,
Magnifies the illumination.

my name is Paull shin

Fears, doubts, excitement...

So many different feelings kept me awake at night. Even the Korean I spoke was a version of very disrespectful street slang only allowed among the lowest classes of the social hierarchy. How could I handle another language?

I was already suffering from culture shock. For someone born and raised in a traditional, conservative culture just beginning to pioneer new ideas, a couple's public display of affection was an astonishing sight.

After a sleepless night, I headed towards Salt Lake City on a Greyhound bus to join my American family.

Past the Californian border, an endless stretch of desert replaced the trees and mountains. I looked around to make sure that I hadn't accidentally gotten on a bus taking me to another country. We crossed into Utah from Nevada, and the sand seemed to turn to snow. Surprised to see snow in such warm weather, I asked the person next to me. He looked at me unable to decide if he should laugh at my joke, or feel insulted. When I explained that I had just arrived in America yesterday, he explained that the white blanket was salt and not snow.

The drive started before the sun rose in the morning, and even after the moon came out, the bus kept going. I couldn't see much of the scenery anymore, but the stars thickly spread across the sky kept me amazed. I had a lot to think about. Will my family accept a foreigner as one of their own? I tried to imagine the family, and wondered how to make a good impression. By the time I reached Salt Lake City, Utah, my father was already waiting for me at the bus station with the rest of the family.

I ran straight into his arms, and all the suppressed emotions finally emerged. Years of separation and longing, years of waiting and anticipation...all disappeared with a warm embrace from my father. His compassion remained constant, and I felt the same sense of comfort and hope I discovered the first time I was introduced to this love.

The beautiful woman standing next to my father welcomed me home with an unexpected hug. My father introduced her as my mother. She had a warm smile on her face, but I remained stiff, not knowing how to respond. I wasn't accustomed to showing affection, especially to strangers, and to hug an American lady was out of the question.

Three boys stood near us, but until my father introduced

them as my brothers, they just stared at me with awe. A slight nudge from my father brought a rushed "hello" out of their mouths. Phillip was eleven, Robert nine, and Howard six.

As we drove through the city, I immediately noticed the order and stability governing the streets. The spacious environment of my surroundings also fascinated me. I came with my own expectations of what America should look like, but to see the desert sand, sagebrush and cactuses not only surprised me, it thoroughly confused me. I was sure Captain Paull lived in America, but I never knew so much of America looked like a desert. When we entered the residential neighborhood, however, I began to see an oasis representing the wealth of America again.

I ignored the giggles and laughter coming from my brothers, and boldly took off my shoes. My mother led me to my room, fully furnished with a bed, a lamp, a desk, and a clothes bureau. She went further to apologize for not preparing extra clothes, because they couldn't estimate my size.

My father's older brother, Charles, and my mother's brother, Lewis, came with their families to welcome me home. It also happened to be Phillip's birthday, so we had much to celebrate. Phillip's friends came to celebrate his birthday, but they spent the majority of the evening examining the new older brother. I felt like a monkey in the zoo.

That night, after all the guests left, I stood in front of my mirror and practiced, "Fa-ther, Fa-ther, Father...Mo-ther...Mother...?"

By this time, I had gotten used to the idea of "Father", but

The gathering of a new family:
From Shin Hobom to Paull Shin…
Posing with my new family before the Christmas tree.
Though awkward and out of place, family was a place of comfort and security,
forming a bond of love.

"Mo-ther"…I couldn't even utter the unfamiliar label to myself without blushing. How could I ever get accustomed to the habit of calling such a beautiful lady my mother, and identifying three blond boys as my brothers?

After my "brothers" had gone to bed, my father and I spent some time alone. We had a lot to catch up on, and many issues to clarify for the future.

"Buckshot, have you thought of an English name for yourself? We can keep Buckshot as a nick name, but Hobom will be difficult to pronounce for most people."

I left my family in Korea, but I couldn't bring myself to abandon my family name. I was old enough to feel the responsibility and pressure of lineage. After some contemplation, I found a solution.

"How about Paull?"

Father knew what I meant. His own name was Ray Paull, which meant I wanted to use his last name as my first, and keep a connection to my biological family with "Shin". Luckily, Paul was a common name, and I would only make a variation on the spelling.

"All right. I would feel honored if you took my name. Next, we have to decide what you want to do, now that you're in America."

"I want to study. It's been my dream to study."

"What a great idea! You're nineteen, right? We'll go to the local high school first thing in the morning."

I didn't know how to respond.

"Uh…I can't. I did not even graduate elementary school, Father."

Understanding the deprivation of my childhood, my father took my hands and reassured me.

"Son, don't worry about it! It's okay!"

We decided to enroll at the nearest elementary school, and ended the long day. Even after my father's words of comfort, I lie down to a worry laden bed. I questioned my ability to adjust in a foreign country, surrounded by unfamiliar faces, and confronted with daily uncertainties.

"How am I going to overcome all the obstacles that lie ahead?"

Getting into school felt like a minor problem when I considered winning the favor of the rest of my adopted family. I tried to convince myself that our relationships could only get better. Instead of victimizing myself, I decided to reflect upon the situation objectively. When someone prepares to adopt a child, they imagine just that, a child. By this time, I was far beyond adolescence, and in no way was I cute. I thought about my father's sacrifice, his love, and his patience. I dedicated myself to helping my family overcome the cultural and emotional shock of accepting a foreign intruder into a perfectly satisfied family.

My father took a risk in adopting me, and now it was my turn to extend the same effort. The rest of the family needed my cooperation in order to feel comfortable with me, and I figured the fastest way to do this was for me to take the first step in assimilating myself as a part of the family.

nine**t**een?!!? i'm sorry…

"My first day of school!"

I woke up with this single thought in mind.

Today, my most treasured dream would become a reality. I looked out the window to see the sun rising over the majestic mountains revealing a combination of beautiful colors.

"Good morning."

I greeted my mother with a thick accent. She smiled and politely asked what I wanted for breakfast, but I didn't know how to answer. After my younger brothers left for school, I ate an all-American-breakfast of bacon, eggs and toast with my father. During the meal I noticed that my mother washed the dishes, so I decided to assume responsibility of washing dishes after that day as my way of initiating a relationship.

In my excitement, I forgot that I had nothing to wear. The

clothes I wore were inappropriate for any occasion in America. I knew my physical features put me at a disadvantage in "blending in" but my attire would make it impossible to make a favorable first impression. While I worried about my outfit, my father walked in with a whole new one. Luckily, he had already thought of my lack of resources, and allowed himself to provide. By the time I walked out of the house, I was a completely different...*man?*...no, student.

We walked into the principal's office of a nearby elementary school, and as soon as my father introduced me as his son from Korea, they asked for my age. The principal didn't even attempt to stifle his laughter when he heard me say nineteen. Disturbed by the unexpected, even rude reaction, my father and I stood there awkwardly waiting for a more appropriate response.

After his amusement subsided, the principal finally said, "I'm sorry, we cannot accept you." He suggested that we try a high school.

My father hid his discouragement, and whistled his way to the junior high school, but uncertainty clouded my optimism, and I couldn't show the same excitement.

"They can't refuse you at the junior high school," my father attempted to reassure me, but once again, I received a similar rejection.

"How old did you say you were?"

"...nineteen years old..."

"I'm sorry..."

"Well then! Straight into high school!" He failed to retain his confidence, and nothing he said could brighten my despair. My father's silence proved that he was in no position to guarantee acceptance.

The high school students and staff were enjoying their lunches when we arrived. We had to go out to the football field to meet the principal, who happened to be feeding watermelon to the football players. Because of Korean stereotypes, I had imagined the principal as a strict, austere administrator behind a desk, but this principal contradicted my assumptions.

My father approached him and explained our situation, but he gave us the preordained answer, "I'm sorry..."

Why had I even bothered to show up? Apparently, the only thing Americans were capable of saying was, "I'm sorry."

"We cannot accept someone who has not received proper elementary or junior high school education."

As if not receiving any proper education was my fault!

My father gave me the courage to transcend reality, and grasp a rainbow behind the clouds. After many years of waiting, I thought I finally arrived at a place where my rainbow was tangible, but now I faced another calamity! To my dismay, I started to cry out loud. I just couldn't hide my frustration and burst into tears.

The principal seemed to sympathize with me, and asked, "Can you explain to me why you're crying?"

I began to stutter my response, "Sir, I came to America to make my dreams come true. They were impossible in Korea...but now all my dreams are disappearing."

"Do you really want to study that badly?"

"Yes! I would do anything if I could just study like other students."

"If you're really serious about studying, there may be a way. You can earn the equivalent of a high school diploma if you pass the Graduate Equivalency Degree exam (GED), and that qualifies you to apply for colleges. Would you like to try that?"

I didn't understand all the details, but to hear a possible solution gave me all the confidence I needed. I shouted, "Yes! I love you!" and hugged him so tightly that he gasped for air.

He was Dr. Kenneth Farr, who provided my second life-altering opportunity. I was immediately introduced to Ms. Evans, an English teacher. She agreed to tutor me two hours a day, starting the next day. After saying our "thank you's", we left the room, ecstatic with the possibilities. We could finally eat a relaxed lunch.

"Now that we've accomplished one thing, we have to go school shopping."

I didn't know how to react as we bought the supplies. I couldn't jump around with excitement like a little child, but I also couldn't protect my dignity by disregarding my gratitude.

During the car ride back home, I felt as if the fleeting rainbow had finally inhabited my heart, pushing out all my worries and premonitions of the inevitable problems I faced.

A gentle squeeze on my hand disturbed my thoughts. I turned to face my father, who quietly said, "I'm glad you're here, my son."

can't take no education for granted

My alarm clock woke me up at six o'clock, and I was in the school library reviewing previous lessons by seven. I waited patiently for Ms Evans' break times to learn more English.

I'm learning…I'm studying. The joy of such a privilege satisfied me, but Ms Evans' personal attention kept me motivated. At four o'clock, the bell never failed to end the school day. I joined the students as they rushed to the buses transporting us back home.

After school, I assigned myself to the responsibility of washing, ironing, and cleaning—chores I never quite escaped. When I remembered that even I was capable of contributing to the family, I didn't mind the time taken away from studying. In retrospect, I can imagine what a nightmare it must have been for my mother. She took care of five men. As a wife, mother, cook, chauffeur…it would have been barbaric of me not to help.

In the meantime, my mother drove me from school to work and anywhere else I needed to go. She tirelessly taught me conventional English and social customs that I needed to understand to be adjusted to American culture. She made great sacrifices for a stranger who suddenly became her son and set the standards of an ideal mother extremely high.

My father kept two careers: a dentist during business hours, and a professor in the evening. Despite his busy schedule, he reserved the hours from 10 p.m. ~ midnight to teach me math, physics, and chemistry. In order to make sure that my father's efforts were not wasted, I reviewed what I learned until I fell asleep around 3 a.m. My three-hour nights started, and lasted till I finished my doctoral dissertation 20 years later. I always waited till the day I could sleep in late, but now that I have the option, I think old age has made me an early bird. My biological clock wakes me up before sunrise.

The English-Korean dictionary helped me when I needed to look up a new word, but it was discouraging to realize how long it took me to finish reading a page. Sometimes, I looked up a word, and found that I didn't understand the definition either. I tried to concentrate on memorizing vocabulary but as soon as I learned a new word, I forgot the previous one. I knew it was a futile effort, but every time I finished learning a new page in the dictionary, I tore the page, burned it, stirred the ashes into water, and drank my dictionary one page at a time. Needless to say, I forgot most of the words and I didn't even have them to use as reference anymore, but how many people can say that they have a whole set of the

English dictionary in their stomach?

There had to be a leak in my brain. No matter how long I studied, the content seemed to slip right out. When I thought I had finally learned something, whatever it was, I didn't remember it in the morning.

Prayers, however childlike they sounded, gave me the confidence to flip another page or move onto the next problem. When everybody was sleeping, I would step out into the backyard at around one or two o'clock in the morning and say a simple prayer:

> *"Dear God,*
> *How are you? I hope you are well. I am alright too. You know God,*
> *I am trying to study this difficult language, and learn high school*
> *course materials. It is very hard, so could you help me get my edu-*
> *cation? Then later, I will help you too."*

There was an orchard nearby in need of workers, so I decided to contribute to my father's financial burden by getting a job. I received $.16 for a bushel of apples, and it took me an average of three hours to pick ten bushels. On one particular Saturday, I spent the whole day climbing up and down trees, until my legs trembled with exhaustion. Too early to end the day, I remembered an old tactic I used when I was younger. I shook the tree, and smiled to see that even the American apples fell right to my feet. I gathered enough to fill 140 bushels, and when I proudly showed my boss, he questioned my ability to produce so many bushels. Before I could finish my explanation, he demanded that I pay for the damages, and chased me out.

I ended up not having to pay for the apples, but I did learn a valuable lesson. I should never shake apples off a tree, because even the slightest imperfection disqualifies the apple as a product in the commercial market.

I attended school every day, encouraged by Mrs. Evans' patience, and Dr. Farr's support, but the students' curiosity grew increasingly irritating. I felt like a circus monkey entertaining his audience. As the exclusive, non-white in the whole school, they referred to me as the "Chinaman" or "fish-eyes". Even if they made an effort to be friendly, I couldn't keep up with the conversation, so they would walk away in frustration, or annoyance. One day, as I was washing my hands in the bathroom, a guy rudely advised, "You're hands aren't getting any whiter, so you might as well give up."

The illusions of an exoticized culture dominated social and religious gatherings. Even the friendly questions contained degrading connotations. "Have you ever seen this fruit before?" "Do you have grapes in your country?" I might have left Korea full of contempt, but treating my country as an inferior nation hurt my own pride.

In Korea, a hierarchical society denied my rights as a citizen. In the land of equality, my ethnicity provoked judgment. I wondered if a time would come when others perceived me for my intrinsic qualities rather than assessing me by superficial inadequacies.

In anticipation of passing the GED exam, I found a job as a

dishwasher at the Hotel Utah to save money for my tuition. Soon after I started, my manager noticed my diligence, and promoted me to a busboy who cleared tables when guests finished their meals.

After a six-hour shift, I came home depleted, but recharged myself to study a few hours before falling asleep. My father's confidence and support gave me purpose, but with such busy schedules, we could go days without seeing each other.

Struggling to survive on three hours of sleep, I confused the sugar and salt, and treated my guests to salty coffee, and sweet steak, at a time when the hotel hosted a convention with over 800 guests. All the guests voiced their complaint. I even fell asleep rolling out the dirty dishes in a cart, and woke up to the screaming of guests. By the time I regained consciousness, I had spilled leftovers all over the guest of honor. The guest looked at me, looked down at the mess, and screamed so loud that I'm sure she woke up any of the hotel guests taking naps. I never knew such a horrendous sound could come out of such a beautiful woman. Her scream certainly attracted the attention of my manager, who rushed out to apologize to the guest, and fired me on the spot.

I gathered my belongings, and walked out, unsure of where I should go next. At the end of a long walk, I found myself on a hill overlooking the whole neighborhood.

"I wonder if all those people out there know what true happiness feels like."

I prayed, "God, why is it that life is such a struggle? Please don't forsake me now, when I need you most."

The clear desert sky exposed an infinity of stars, each shining uniquely. Looking up to such magnificence made me realize I still had much more to be thankful for.

My manager called me the next morning, asking me to return to work. He explained that firing me was the only way to appease the guest's anger, and demonstrate the value of each guest. Another busy day began, but today, I was thankful for my challenges.

The next fall arrived, and so did my test date. Everyone wished me luck, but I knew I needed more than just luck. I took the test in a frantic convulsion. My shirt was soaked with sweat by the end of the first half, and I had broken my pencil lead several times by the end.

Once I finished the test, whether I passed or not became a secondary concern. For the time being, completion gave me all the pleasure I needed. I doubted myself, but at the same time, I kept my expectations high. At the end of an anxious week, my mother brought an envelope to my room.

I ripped through the envelope to reveal my results, and my eyes lingered on the words spelling out "pass". My heart stopped while I checked to make sure I wasn't hallucinating. I confirmed my sanity, but my heart couldn't resume its normal pulse. Even as my sweat and tears blurred the ink, I refused to let go of the piece of paper. I had worked so hard and long to see these results.

Those who wished me luck with empty encouragements returned genuine congratulations. Even my father rushed home from work to show me how proud he was of my accomplishment.

In June, I graduated from Olympus High School. Dr. Farr and Mrs. Evans were especially happy to see me move on. They always hold a place in my heart, as ones who played a pivotal role in my life. When everyone rejected me, they gave me a chance, and when everyone laughed at my ignorance, they gave me an encouraging smile.

Walking down the aisle with the other high school graduates was a very humbling experience, but it gave me pride knowing that I could call them colleagues, especially when I saw the delight in my parents' eyes. My father couldn't contain his warm tears, so I shared in his joy.

Feeling the satisfaction of reward after a period of almost fruitless efforts invalidated the setbacks and stress of preparation. I developed a fixation on my lack of education, but now I could let go of all the shame, because I held the equivalent of a high school diploma in my hands. My greatest appreciation stemmed from knowing that I didn't disappoint my mother and father. Their provision and constant support displayed their approval, and helped me feel accepted.

Throughout my studies, and for the rest of my career, I always remembered my father's simple yet sincere encouragements that kept me focused and motivated: "My son, I believe in you." He gave me the courage to believe in myself, and believe I could find a way to accomplish what I set my heart on.

If he believed in me, then there was no reason for me to doubt myself.

my first date with miss america

Passing the GED gave me the courage to have confidence in other aspects of my life. However, the challenges I faced in college proved to be much harder to conquer than the ones I overcame in high school. At the University of Utah, confusing seminars and a lack of racial variation discouraged me, but I tried to ignore the disparities. My father noticed my struggles and helped in every way possible. However, knowing the burden I imposed on my adopted family, I wanted to support myself financially.

In order to include all my chores as a son, a student and a busboy in a hotel restaurant, I continued to keep my sleeping time limited to no more than three hours a night. Despite the added responsibilities, I felt more at peace. I witnessed the power of money when I took my brothers out on the weekends, and found that they preferred me as the independent older brother than their housemaid.

Even in my strictly routine and monotonous life, I came across a couple of unforgettable incidents.

My mother learned that Koreans liked rice, so she bought some rice and made rice pudding for the family...mostly in an attempt to accommodate my preferences. I was so grateful for her consideration that I was prepared to compliment the taste, regardless of the truth. I enjoyed the novelty of the experience, but not only was it different from what I was accustomed to, I have to admit that I found the texture disturbing and the flavor nauseating! Since I was determined to show my appreciation, I swallowed hard and said, "Yum!" I figured if I could hurry up and finish the pot, the torture would end sooner. Too bad my mother misinterpreted my hastiness as a sign to make another pot full of rice pudding.

"I'll leave it in the fridge for you, so you can have some whenever you want!"

"Thank you so much! I bet it's just as good as the first pot!"

After a few pots, I realized that I had to come clean with my mother before she made another pot.

My mother was surprised when I refused to eat the pudding one day and asked, "Don't you like the rice anymore?"

"Mother, we just don't eat rice like this in Korea."

I hoped she wouldn't take it personally, but my mother eventually understood, and this incident helped us break down some cultural barriers.

In the mornings, my mother would ask if I wanted some

eggs, but out of politeness, I refused because they were such expensive delicacies in Korea when I was growing up. After a while, she just assumed I didn't like eggs, and stopped asking. Even to this day, I avoid eating eggs as much as possible. Out of habit I suppose...

Late one night as I was waiting for a bus, I came across a bum covered in filth and wreaking of alcohol. He fell and hit his head on the cement, so he was bleeding. I couldn't ignore my feeling of empathy, so I carried him to a nearby shelter. I turned around to leave, but he grabbed my hand and thanked me. In his twenty-six years of homelessness no one had ever helped him to a bed before. After his wife and son left, he spent twenty-six years alone.

Daylight drew near as I walked in the house, and my father scolded me for the first time. He asked me to ignore my "good Samaritan" impulses because some people on the streets were untrustworthy and dangerous. But I kept thinking that if I hadn't met the kind Captain Paull, I could have been the harmful drunk people want to avoid.

My father's suggestion caught me by surprise one day.

"If you just study and work too much, not only will you burn yourself out, you'll regret it when you're older. Why don't you date and meet some girls? I've already arranged for you to go out with the prettiest girl in town. She's the daughter of a friend from dental school. Her name's Charlotte, I've already made prepaid dinner reservations at the Hotel Utah restaurant, and here are two movie tickets. Make sure you take her to the movies after dinner."

Blond hair, blue eyes, sparkling white teeth, and a flawless figure—she looked like she had jumped right out of a picture and showed up at my doorstep.

"Have a good time! If you come back too early, we won't let you in!"

My knees felt locked in place as I walked stiffly to Charlotte's car and stumbled in.

Charlotte initiated the conversations, but I made minimal contributions.

I gave one of two answers for the rest of the evening.

If she asked, "Do you want to visit Korea sometime?"

I answered, "No."

"Are you having a hard time keeping up in school?"

"Yes."

"Is English is a difficult language to learn?"

"Yes."

"You must miss Korean food."

"Yes."

She tried so hard to ease the awkwardness. When we walked into the hotel restaurant, all eyes turned to us. Some recognized Charlotte as the Utah State Queen of Rodeo, but most of the stares were directed towards me, to let me know of their disapproval.

My manager ran out to witness the miracle himself.

"How did this happen?" he asked. Throughout the whole dinner, he kept returning to wait on us, but I had a feeling he was more interested in my pretty date than her escort.

Charlotte stopped trying to include me in the conversation

My first date: the beauty queen
Blond hair, blue eyes, a warm heart and a generous nature made Charlotte a timeless beauty.

and started talking about herself. I spent dinner listening to her talk, completely absorbed by her beauty. She possessed more than just physical beauty. I was impressed by her unsuccessful efforts to lighten the mood, and her kindness was undeserved. After dinner we welcomed the dessert, all of which was prepaid by my father.

Then Charlotte inquired, "Where do you want to go next?"

"Uh...I don't care..."

"There has to be some place in particular you'd like to go."

I completely lost my ability to speak. I felt two movie tickets at my fingertips, but the words just didn't come out.

She asked again, "So...any suggestions?"

"Why don't we go home?"

"Are you sure? You really want to go home?"

"Yes."

Startled, and probably a little insulted, she didn't know what else to say, except a quick, "Fine."

While my fingers hesitated on the movie tickets in my pocket, I even forgot to open the doors for her. Charlotte continued with her attempts at a conversation, but I kept my answers simple with "yes" and "no".

My father answered the door, shocked to see me back so soon. When I told him what happened, he hit his head in disbelief, and shook his head with amusement. That night he gave me an important lecture on the rules of dating.

"First, you treat the lady like a queen. Second, you never take her home before midnight. It's not a matter of how much you like her it's the man's responsibility and duty to obey these rules."

A week later, Charlotte called me. This time, she was in control, and asked me to dress casually. My father drove me to her house, and we went to a place called Crazy Bar Ranch.

"Do you know how to ride a horse?"

Of course I'd never tried, but with a sudden rush of confidence I thought, "How hard could it be?" so I replied ambiguously with, "It's not that hard."

Other people rested on the horse so casually, but when I actually climbed up, I felt extremely vulnerable, and even a little airsick. I needed to catch up to Charlotte, who had started ahead of me, but I didn't know how to command my horse to move. I remembered what I'd seen in the movies, so I gave a hard pull on the reins. However, the horse misunderstood my command, and kicked up his front legs. Unprepared for the sudden leap, I flew off the horse, and fell hard enough to leave a permanent imprint of my bottom on the ground.

"Paull! Are you all right? You should have told me you didn't know how to ride a horse!"

Charlotte gave me a quick lesson on riding and we enjoyed the rest of the day without too many disasters. When I woke up the next morning, I understood the meaning of "every bone in my body aching." I started to feel sorry for the fearless cowboys in the movies.

After our disastrous dates, we became good friends— visiting, and writing letters. At school, however, I kept a safe distance. Whenever I saw her coming in my direction, I found a place to hide before she could notice me. I didn't want people to think she was associated with me in any way. Our correspondence ended when I went to Japan as a missionary the following year.

During my time in Japan, I received an unexpected letter from Charlotte, asking me to meet her in Tokyo while she stopped by on her tour as the reigning Miss America. Under missionary regulations I should have refused, but I received special permission from the mission president, allowing me to meet her in Tokyo.

She looked even more beautiful than before. Perhaps the glamour of her title gave Charlotte an added sense of splendor and elegance.

My missionary partner followed us as a chaperone, but his supervision was completely unnecessary, because in the crowded restaurant, everyone watched us with admiration. We tried our best to ignore the stares, and carried on with our own conversation.

"Paull, what do you think about me being Miss America?"

"To be honest, I'm scared for you."

"What do you mean?"

"I'm afraid that the fame and attention will feed you with false realities, and end with detrimental effects on your future."

"Thank you for your honesty, but I can assure you, that won't happen to me. I'm just an ordinary girl, looking for a more wholesome life. I'm not interested in the fame or glory."

We ignored my partner's disapproving glare, and warmly

shook hands before parting.

While I was back in America continuing my education, I received a wedding invitation from Charlotte. Just as she promised, she was pursuing an ordinary life as the wife of a high school teacher.

Many years later, I received another invitation to her home, where she led the wholesome life as a wife, and a mother of six. She no longer possessed the head-turning attractiveness I remembered, but her beauty as a person never diminished as she enjoys her life as a plump grandmother, serving her community and family.

my first love

One Sunday morning, I visited the Shibuya Branch in Tokyo, and I immediately noticed a woman who stood out from the rest. Her perfectly proportioned features and elegant kimono (Japanese traditional clothing) separated her from the ordinary housewives. Even her two children showed signs of royalty. The effects of the war heightened her beauty, and all eyes focused on her every move. I toured four churches on Sundays, but every time I thought of the Shibuya Branch, her image occupied my thoughts.

My first duty and obligation in Japan was as a missionary, but I couldn't control my emotions. Every time I saw her, I felt a renewed sense of exhilaration, but her beauty didn't capture my heart. The loneliness in her eyes made me vulnerable.

As an illegitimate child of the royal family, her birth disgraced the imperial family. They sent her into exile in Shodoshima of the Shikoku Islands to be raised by a surrogate mother. Dismissal was the most expedient cover. Despite her illegitimacy, the royal family could not totally discard her existence. They provided a governess to educate her through high school, and until she finished her education, she was not allowed on the mainland. Once she acquired the proper qualifications for higher learning, she entered the Gakushuin Academy, a college for nobility. During her senior year at the college, she won first prize in the national Haiku—a traditional form of Japanese poetry—contest, sponsored by the emperor. The emperor came out to present the award, but concealed her identity in fear of scandal.

Towards the time of her graduation, she met her betrothed, an army major, and married. After having two children, her husband fell victim to an unfortunate car accident, and left her a widow. The tragic accident finally freed her from years of control and domination from the family that renounced her.

She was Ito Shizue, my first love, and the cause of much suffering—eight years older than me, the mother of two children, but most controversial of all, the blood in her veins represented a nation that tortured my homeland. I wanted to believe that love is oblivious to conditions and indifferent to reason. It transcends all boundaries, and ignores manipulation.

Was it a coincidence or fate? My companion and I were assigned to lead a Bible study at Shizue's home once a week.

Spending so much time with her exposed even more admirable qualities of Shizue. Her willingness to serve, her warmth and compassion all added to her beauty. She possessed

Broken love, first love
My first love ended in heartache and disappointment
but she remains a memory preserved by a picture.

the modesty of a Japanese woman, but her ability to share her painful past while contradicting her tears with a smile, claimed my attention.

Every moment I spent with her diminished the emptiness in my own heart, and I couldn't even attempt to restrain the powerful current drowning all sense of logic and self-discipline. I knew there was one thing I had to do before our relationship progressed any further. Because of my loyalty to the regulations as a missionary, I confessed my feelings to the Mission President, and he reassigned me to another city far away.

I actually thought my feelings would subside if I didn't see her, but I proved myself wrong. After a long battle with my conscience, I gave up and wrote a letter. It's amazing what you can convey in writing, because I found the courage to express emotions I never dared to speak of.

We exchanged a few letters, and Shizue finally visited me in Okagama City. During her stay, we took a trip to the island she grew up on, chaperoned by my companion, of course, and confessed our love for each other.

There was a minor disturbance. After brief hesitation, Shizue rolled back her sleeves to reveal a scar caused by radiation from the atomic bomb. When the United States dropped the atomic bomb on August 6, 1945, Shizue was near Hiroshima, and the radiation caused cancer.

"The doctors tell me it's not fatal."

"If the doctors believe you're healthy, then you shouldn't worry. My commitment as a missionary is almost up. I'd like you to join me in America."

"What about my children?"

"Of course they'll join us. I'll raise them as my own. Don't you think they can find more opportunities in America?"

Crystal tears dropped from her eyes, but she never neglected a smile to express her gratitude.

My companion walked ahead, giving us the freedom to hold hands.

The year of 1958 came to an end, and so did my time as a missionary. I parted with my acquaintances, and board a ship leaving Japan. Many friends came out to watch me depart, but Shizue was not with the crowd because we agreed to keep our relationship as discreet as possible out of respect for the other missionaries. I gazed out at the disappearing island, and silently bid a temporary farewell to Shizue.

As soon as I returned to America, I persuaded my father to support our marriage, and sent an invitation to Japan for Shizue and her children. I was drafted into the United States Army for two years and moved to Texas for military training, but we continued our correspondence.

The intense training and relentless discipline seemed like a manifestation of hell, but Shizue's letters transported me into a place of refuge, and revitalized my courage to survive another day. Until one day, her consistent letters suddenly stopped without an explanation. Frustrated by the abrupt silence, I called her in Japan.

"Ito Shizue died of cancer," was the reply from her uncle in

Osaka.

"That's not possible!"

My own disbelief muted the remaining details, and cut off my supply of air.

"What about the children?"

"A relative has taken custody of them."

I woke up with swollen eyes until my whole body protested out of dehydration. Time was my only medicine. After a few days, I regained my appetite, and after a few weeks, I woke up feeling rested.

Who said that a man never forgets his first love...or that a first love never lasts...?

These superstitions must have compromised my relationship with Shizue, but does everything really happen for a reason? I did learn that one could truly love and embrace another regardless of background, origin or nationality.

aunt margaret's inheritance

On the journey home from Japan, after completing my mission term, I chose to travel by ship from Yokohama to San Francisco.

Everyone on the ship had a date, partner, or a group of friends to associate with, except me… During mealtimes, however, I noticed that nobody appeared to accompany a certain grandmother. She must have also noticed me, because she started walking in my direction, said "Hello," and pointing to the empty seat next to mine, she asked, "Is this seat taken?"

"No, it's all yours!" I exclaimed. For the next two weeks, we kept each other company. The two of us made an odd pair. I looked young enough to be her grandson, but I didn't look related to her in any way. Into the second week of our acquaintance, she asked me to call her Aunt Margaret. She told me stories of her past experiences, and I had some adventures of my own to share. Ever since her fiancé broke the engagement and her heart at age nine-teen, Aunt Margaret never allowed herself to feel that kind of love towards another man.

After retiring from 42 years as an English teacher at a junior high school, she set out to tour the world, and I met her on her way back from Japan. A mutual loneliness allowed us to open up and feel companionship in each other. The two weeks flew by, and before we knew it, we were making promises to keep in touch through letters. She wrote me about two to three times a week, while I barely kept up with one. Instead of feeling neglected, she patiently waited for my replies. She even corrected my grammatical errors and sent the modified version back to me.

When I traveled with my friends while I was stationed in Germany as a soldier in the United States Army, I used her travel journals as reference to decide my course of travel. In one of her letters, she suggested that I go to Oberammergau to see the famous "Oberammergau Passion Play", the first theater production recounting the life of Christ, which has been showing every ten years since the early seventeenth century.

I immediately replied to invite her to Germany, so she could see The Passion Play with me. She gladly accepted my invitation, and joined me shortly after in Germany. Thirty years ago, Aunt Margaret had already seen the play, but she welcomed the opportunity to refresh her memory. She was delighted to see that even after so many years, the content and overall presentation remained the same despite the different actors. Since I owned a car at the time, we had the freedom to travel around West Germany and neighboring countries. Considering her age, I feared the traveling might strain Aunt Margaret's health, but I was the one who lagged behind. We even traveled to Cardigan, Wales, Aunt Margaret's birth place, and I went as her guest. After my time in the army, I visited Aunt Margaret in Ohio. It felt like going home to my own grandmother's place in Geumchon.

In the spring of 1962, I received a call from Aunt Margaret's lawyer, informing me of her death. I rushed out to capture one last moment with an amazing friend. When I arrived at the funeral ceremony, a young couple introduced to me as a distant relative of Aunt Margaret blatantly glared at me, so I assumed they disapproved of my ethnicity. It was a small, quiet ceremony in the presence of a few friends and students.

While I was still mourning her departure, the lawyer asked to speak with me privately. I followed him to a room where the unfriendly couple waited.

"Ms. Margaret Edwards has left her house, a cabin by Lake Michigan, and her grand piano to you, Mr. Shin."

I had no idea Aunt Margaret had included me in her will, let alone leave me such a considerable fortune. Now I understood the young couple's hostility, and said to them, "I have no interest in Aunt Margaret's wealth and possessions. I'm satisfied with my memories of the adventures and love we shared. If you want, I'll let you deal with it in any way you want."

Everyone seemed shocked at my forfeit of the inheritance. They recovered soon enough to create a contract to document my statement to transfer the inheritance. The couple suddenly dropped their unwelcoming attitudes, and insisted on treating me to dinner.

Thinking back I wonder, "Maybe I should've kept the piano. I could treasure the precious instrument, molded to Aunt Margaret's fingertips ..."

I still remember her advice:

"I regret turning my back on love. Nobody deserves the punishment of living alone. If I'd only known...Paull, you survived a lonely and difficult childhood. Promise me you'll find someone and live happily together."

a Promise I never forgot

Relaxation and a sense of homecoming replaced the anxiety I felt entering the San Francisco harbor four years ago. I embraced the sight of the Golden Gate Bridge with open arms.

My parents and three brothers waited for me. My father and mother ran towards me to make sure that all my body parts remained intact, and everyone welcomed my safe return. Something else waited for me at home, but my parents allowed me to absorb the joy of arrival before they laid a letter from Uncle Sam on my shoulders.

As I unpacked my things, my father walked in to give me the letter.

"This is a letter from the U.S. government. A draft notice from the Army..."

He seemed to have expected such a notice, and struggled to

give me an explanation.

"What do you think? You can still continue your education when you return. If we keep an optimistic attitude, this can be an opportunity for you to improve your English, and a great experience for you."

I felt relieved knowing that this wouldn't affect my education. "America has opened up a new life for me. It's time to repay some of my debt."

After a two-year absence, less than two weeks later, I packed my bags again. I reported to my military duty at Fort Carlson, in Colorado, and changed into the uniform they gave me. I felt like a houseboy all over again.

Soldiers assigned to Korea trained in Colorado, and those assigned to West Germany trained in Texas. I hoped to train in Colorado, but to my disappointment, my destiny led me to Fort Hood in Texas.

Any desire to sleep was replaced by uncertainties. Could I really behave appropriately as an American soldier? For so many years I lived in the battalions where the living and the dead coexisted, but even after witnessing so many soldiers returning incompletely, the queasiness from seeing blood never diminished. I remembered Lieutenant Booth's struggle with bigotry, and questioned my own predicament.

"What will my commanding officer be like?"

The worst weather condition greeted me in Texas, but the training regimes never took the weather into consideration.

After a long week of training and military meals, a few of my white friends and I decided to enjoy some good civilian food. We agreed to be a little superfluous and arrived at a fancy restaurant with chandeliers and a maître'd waiting for us at the door. In my excitement, I forgot one minor detail. Here in the south, severe segregation still existed. On the door of the restaurant, a sign indicated that I wasn't welcome.

"The Whites Only."

I hesitated before the sign thinking, perhaps the sign was intended for other minorities, but I wasn't exactly white either. My friends noticed my uncertainty, but convinced me that the sign wasn't meant for me. They dragged me inside assuming that the managers would see our uniforms and overlook the minor detail out of compassion for the hungry soldiers. They were wrong. The manager spotted me right away, and angrily demanded, "What the hell are you doing here?"

Before I could protest, he picked me up by my collar, dragged me across the restaurant while all the other customers watched, and dumped me outside on the concrete floor like a bag of garbage. The combination of humiliation, pain, confusion, and anger made the tears rip through my heart.

All my friends acted out against the inequity, and walked out of the restaurant to comfort me. By the time we returned to the base, all the dining halls had closed for the day. So that evening, our hunger for extravagance left us starving through the night.

I hardly slept that night, but my empty stomach had nothing to do with the insomnia this time. I sat up on my bed and gazed into the starry horizon as if the stars could map my future.

Perhaps the manager wanted to prove to other customers their emphasis on segregation, and wanted people to feel safe and reassured about coming to an all white restaurant.

When I woke up in the morning, my pillow was soaked with tears. I was putting my life on hold for a country that couldn't see past my exterior. Even in a uniform, I was considered less than American, even less than human for extreme racists. Where do I really belong? I cried out, "God if you're there, please answer this: why am I subject to discrimination everywhere I go?"

I came to this country prepared to embrace it as my home, but I kept getting rejected no matter how hard I tried. Everywhere I went, people kept reminding me of my inferior status, and instilling a sense of fear over confidence. I felt a burst of indignation crying out, "Someday, I will serve you."

In my morning prayer, however, I established this vow as a personal goal, and accepted the challenge as a promise to myself rather than an act of vengeance towards the restaurant regulations. Rather than bitterness, I turned to serve.

I may have been treated with disrespect but I wanted to offer myself as a public servant, attacking the very policies that allowed such injustice, and eliminating the margins for segregation. Despite the exasperation I felt, I wanted to demonstrate my admiration for this country, and promote the need for unity. Dissention undermines the foundation of America, and misrepresents the product of liberty. Above all, I wanted to replace discrimination with compassion and seek a chance to serve with love.

A certain American idol also trained in Texas. The name,

Elvis Presley should ring a bell. No one expected him to survive the strict routines of training beginning at five a.m. every day. However, he proved everyone wrong, and even made some valuable contributions of his own. He improved the bathroom facilities, built a game room at his own expense, and performed for us every once in a while. We even sailed to Germany on the same ship.

The basic training period ended in eight weeks, and we separated into specialized fields. I preferred operating the large tanks, but my platoon leader assigned me to work in the company office to learn office administration. Because I completed all my given tasks with speed and efficiency, he saw my values, and handpicked me to work for his cousin, Charles Trinkle, the army chaplain in Germany. I had the advantage of my training as a houseboy.

After the second eight weeks of training, our unit, the Second Armored Division was ordered to depart for Europe. In order to take a ship to West Germany, we took a train to New York. Spending three days on a train to reach another city helped me reassess the magnitude of the country. The facilities on the boat taking us to Germany, however, needed improvement.

Our cabins were too small to begin with, but in order to conserve space, and increase the number of passengers, four beds were stacked, one on top of another, leaving barely enough room to lie still. Many people woke up with complaints of hitting their heads on the upper bunk, and I constantly feared that my bed frame would give in and flatten the guy beneath me. For ten days,

I alternated between the suffocating room and the chilly ocean air, until we finally arrived in Bremenhaven, West Germany.

I got off the ship and joined a long line of soldiers waiting to get on a truck to transport them to the next destination, when a captain approached me and asked,

"Are you Private Paull Shin?"

"Yes Sir!" I boldly answered.

"I'm Charles Trinkle, the army chaplain. Please follow me to my car."

As our car drove away, I looked back to see the image of soldiers helping each other into the trucks. A soldier pulling his friend up into the truck reminded me of my own fortune many years ago. I could almost project myself back to the day I first climbed into an American G.I. truck in Korea.

I wondered if I could lend a helping hand out to the war-torn citizens, and offer as much assistance as I received...

Major Trinkle's voice brought me back to reality.

"My cousin's a very good judge of character, and he thinks very highly of you. I think we'll get along."

freedom behind wheels

Even in the brief encounter, I could sense Major Trinkle's unquestionable integrity. The thought of living in another unfamiliar country forced me to concentrate on adjusting to my surroundings. West Germany seemed almost unaffected by the destructions of war. Unlike Japan, a sense of peace dominated in the balance between nature and artistic architecture. The past few months turned into a blur in my mind. Although I had traveled through three continents, listening to complex instructions of my responsibilities for the following two years overwhelmed me with inadequacy, and I feared that I would disgrace Lieutenant VanDeeter.

As the Chaplain's assistant, I was promoted to a corporal, which meant no more military drills, and I even worried less about conflicts arising because of my ethnicity. The Chaplain's office not only provided religious advice and guidance, we also oversaw every moral aspect of all the enlisted men. This entailed that we organize special lectures and programs to encompass a very versatile education ranging from spiritual growth to resisting the urge to steal.

I always performed most of my duties with the accuracy and efficiency expected of me. Organizing notes, running errands...but writing letters always scarred my self-esteem. After writing a letter, I always expected a burst of laughter to erupt from the chaplain's office as he read through my mistakes. However, instead of belittling me for my incompetence, he patiently corrected them and helped me improve my writing.

When the chaplain and his family left on a vacation, he asked me to watch over their dog. I didn't know much about canines, but I considered it a relatively simple task. I must have given him too much food the first day, because he barely ate for the next couple days. I panicked, and found a solution. I thought the dog preferred human food to regular dog food, so I fed him steak for the next few days. Again, he grew tired of the same food, and stopped enjoying it. Everyone likes ice cream, so I wondered if dogs felt the same way. Just as I suspected, the dog wagged his tail to show how much he loved the sweet treat. He licked every drop of the ice cream I fed him until the chaplain returned.

A few days later, Chaplain Trinkle called me in a very concerned voice.

"What on earth did you feed our dog while we were gone?"

"Uh...just steak and ice cream..."

"Hahaha! You've totally spoiled him! He refuses to even look at his generic dog food!"

One day, a tall skinny German boy called out to me while I was working at the base.

"Hey Mister! Do you think you can take me for a ride on one of the planes?"

"But I'm not a pilot."

"You can ask a pilot to take us for a ride."

He had some audacity for a twelve-year-old, and I didn't want to disappoint this kid, so I asked a pilot for a favor. Surprisingly, he agreed, and the three of us took a tour of the town for the next thirty minutes. The ecstatic boy got off the plane and promised to become a pilot when he grew up. The boy's courage determined his career, and my willingness to help him reminded me of the value of small favors.

Because of my kindness to him, he invited me to his home to meet his family and even introduced me to his beautiful sister. I took her out to an opera, but I'm ashamed to admit that I fell asleep. Hurt and insulted, she vowed to never date a barbaric American soldier again.

Twenty years later, in 1980, I took my family to visit the home of Major Walter Engelhardt, a squadron leader in the German Air Force. I felt honored to have taken part in establishing a childhood dream.

When I decided I wanted the freedom of traveling around Europe by car, I went to a nearby dealer, and demanded to speak with the manager. The employees directed me to the very top floor of the building, so I climbed the steps to the manager's office. The manager gave me a list of recommendations, but they were all a few thousand dollars out of my price range. Frustrated by my refusals, the manager asked, "What kind of car do you want?"

I looked out the window, and spotted an old car sitting in the lot.

"How much for that one?" I asked.

"If you wanted that, why'd you come all the way up here? I don't even know if that car's for sale, or if it still runs."

"I don't care. How much?"

"Well, I suppose about $300…"

"I don't have that much. All I have is $175, and I still need to purchase insurance, so how about $120?"

I think he was surprised by my boldness, but the good-hearted manager accepted my offer, and we sealed the deal with a very informal hand-shake. I acquired my very first Mercedes Benz.

I took the velvet cloth from disposed church pews to cover the seats, and shined the car till it looked like Hitler's escort vehicle. This car carried me all across Europe, and transformed me into a very cultured, sophisticated man. I met Michelangelo in Rome, experienced the Renaissance in Florence, and captured the timeless art pieces at the Louvre museum in Paris. Vienna, Venice, Verona, England, Scandinavia…I even participated in the festival of San Fermin (running of the bulls), and tried running away from the bulls let loose on the streets.

What fun is a vacation when you go alone? Of course I had friends accompanying me to enhance my explorations. I still keep in touch with a couple of them.

My Mercedes served me well, and when it came time for me to leave, I sold the car for $250. Impressed with German automobiles, I purchased a brand new Volkswagen to ship it back to America for $750. In congruence with my profit on the Mercedes, I sold the VW for $900 to my father-in-law after I got married.

My two-year service ended, and I was scheduled to return home. Others rejoiced in their freedom, and anticipation of reunions, but I remained burdened by the thought of battling those I made an effort to protect. In the uniform, I built my confidence as an American, and better prepared myself to face the inevitable challenges waiting for me.

Thirty-three years later, the Trinkle couple visited me in Seattle, and we recounted our memories of Germany.

failed attempts

I first met Heidrun when she came to the chaplain's office for an interview. She came in response to an advertisement seeking a pianist. Not only was she a woman of talent, she was also beautiful. Heidrun played the piano during the worship services and Bible studies, and in a chapel full of rugged soldiers, Heidrun stood out like an angel, descended from heaven. She was an idol of admiration.

As the chaplain's assistant, I had the privilege of escorting this angel to the morning and evening services, and with the excuse of improving my German and her English, we spent additional hours watching movies or communicating over dinner. To me, music was nothing but a form of entertainment. I didn't even know what all the lines and dots stood for, but Heidrun personalized the art for me. We enjoyed each other's company, but there were instigators encouraging us to develop our platonic relationship.

Heidrun's father was a council member of Ulm. Some racial tension existed in Germany, but I found favor in his eyes, and her father became the strongest perpetrator in our relationship. Her mother played the role of a quintessential housewife, always occupied with housework, prepared authentic German meals whenever I visited, and she always found time to bake me specialties. We spent weekends with her family, touring the neighboring cities and countries, even before Heidrun and I became romantically involved.

Marrying Heidrun seemed practical and convenient, so I approached the subject rather casually.

"Why don't we get married?" I asked.

I remember her answer being close to a "Why not?"

Heidrun greeted the guests and played a beautiful hostess at our engagement party, but I tried to remain immobile, afraid that the guests might hear my irregular heartbeat or notice my shaky limbs. We had about 20 guests, consisting of friends and family who came to congratulate our engagement. My anxiety came from more than just the superficial aspects of the event. I feared the obstacles we would face as a couple. How do we fight a defenseless battle?

Once I was discharged from the army, I returned to America to be with my family in Salt Lake City, and immediately transferred to Brigham Young University, where I received a scholarship. Heidrun finished her undergraduate education in Germany, and entered the graduate program at the University of Utah. In America, we were confronted with an irreconcilable dilemma. As soon as I stepped out of my uniform, I fell from a confident, respected soldier, to a struggling, insecure foreign student. Heidrun saw the discrimination I suffered, and recognized my mother's concern, who still preferred that I marry within my own ethnicity. My mother's disapproval of Heidrun, forced her to stay with a family friend.

Heidrun's father, on the other hand, continued to pressure me to rush our marriage, but I pushed their patience too long. I wanted to wait till I received my college diploma, which required too much time. Heidrun fit into the mainstream society while I remained unaccepted. I was busy securing my own future, and Heidrun met another man I couldn't even compete with. Her father had lost control over the matter.

I was physically exhausted from keeping up in school, and emotionally devastated with betrayal. When I heard the news of her marriage, I tried to eliminate the memories we shared by destroying anything related to, or reminding me of Heidrun. Ripping apart pictures and throwing away souvenirs temporarily diminished the pain.

Between my job and school, I kept myself busy as a cure for the scar Heidrun left. A year passed by before I finally decided to heed my mother's advice and seek a Korean wife. I considered going to Korea, but I anticipated the prejudice against an adoptee who didn't even understand his native tongue, and I decided to search in America. I heard of a Korean student at Temple College in Texas, and went to meet her, but quickly found that she already had a wide selection of Korean admirers to choose from. I didn't even have the courage to approach her.

Unlike today, the only place to find a concentrated Korean population was Hawaii, so I wrote a letter to the Korean Consulate in Hawaii.

Dear Consul General,

My name is Shin Hobom. I am 27 years old and currently a college student majoring in political science. I want to marry a Korean woman, but do not know anyone. I am asking for your help.

I would really appreciate it if you could provide a few women for me to meet when I arrive in Hawaii this August.

Before I received a reply to my very obscure letter, I flew to Hawaii, and showed up before the Consul General. To my surprise, he had already prepared three women.

The first woman I met, was a Hawaiian born, second generation Korean. She had long hair and a great figure. Anyone could easily be attracted to her appearance, but her demanding attitude intimidated me. She went out of her way to make sure I opened all the doors, pulled out her chairs, and took responsibility as a man. However, her inability to speak Korean prevented me from asking her out on another date.

I met my second date the next evening. She transferred to the University of Hawaii from Sookmyung Women's University in

Korea, to study chemistry. Nothing about her appearance attracted me, but her refined manners and shy behavior felt comfortable. She politely covered her mouth when she laughed, kept her legs respectfully crossed, and accommodated my weak attempt to integrate Korean in our conversation. I felt encouraged when she agreed to see me again the next day.

On our second date, I showed up with a bouquet of flowers.

"Flowers! Nobody's given me flowers before!"

I found the awkward way she accepted the flowers appealing, almost endearing. For our third date, I decided to treat her with more thought and attention. We met at the International District near the Waikiki Beach, ate a traditional Hawaiian dinner, and explored the streets. I paid close attention to learn what she liked, and bought her a fountain pen, accompanied by a costly broche. I wanted to buy her a ring right away, but I didn't want to scare her off already. As we parted, I looked for an opportunity to make a move of affection, but she courteously bid me good-bye, and turned around. The sense of dissatisfaction intrigued me, so I formally proposed.

"I have to return to school now, but I was wondering if you would marry me."

"Us, marry? How? We're still students!"

"I know...we could finish our education as a couple."

"But... You can hardly speak Korean...how could you consider yourself Korean?"

Color flooded my face, and my embarrassment turned to fury. She didn't even appreciate my effort.

"I'm sorry… I don't see how we could communicate…"

To her, I was nothing but an ignorant adoptee, abandoned by my own parents. Emotionally and financially crippled, I left Hawaii the next morning. I wasted all my hard earned money on a fruitless expedition, leaving me vulnerable to doubt and grief, once again. The pain of unrequited love never diminishes with repetition.

"God, is there really someone out there you have prepared for me? Can she love and cherish me as a husband and friend? From this point, I'm counting on you to provide."

proposal at the grave yard

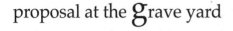

The only way I could forget the pain and torment of rejection was to generate all of my energy towards graduating. I took 18 credits per semester, while working longer hours. I hardly gave myself enough time to sleep.

One of my childhood dreams included becoming a doctor. At age eight, I caught malaria. Unable to seek help, I lie in a delirious state on a street corner, and by the fourth day of my illness, I fell unconscious. The street cleaner reported a dead beggar, but when the police came, they found a pulse, and took me to the hospital. I woke up to the face of a doctor, and wanted to become one to help other children like me.

No matter how hard I studied, however, I could not prevent myself from failing subjects in math and science. To fulfill requirements, I took biology, zoology, and math...and failed all three. I turned to my advisor, hoping to find some sort of solution. He gently suggested that I focus on my stronger subjects to choose my major. History and politics came easily...or easier than math and science. I declared political science as my major, to coincide with my promise to become a politician, and history as my minor, because I never wanted to give up my dream to become a teacher.

In order to stay closer to campus, I rented a small, basement room for $17 a month. It was the cheapest I could find, and I furnished it with very frugal accommodations. I used bed sheets as curtains, and since I didn't have any cooking facilities, I lived off of condensed soup. If I placed a can of Campbell's Chicken Noodle Soup on the heating duck before I left for school in the morning, I could add hot water, and eat it with bread by the time I returned. It was a way to conserve time and money.

During my senior year, I used all my spare time studying for the Foreign Service Examination. I failed the first time, but passed my second time around. Passing helped me regain confidence in my efforts and abilities.

Shortly after my test results arrived, I received a letter from the government, congratulating me on my success. I was now eligible to work as a Foreign Service Agent.

My spirits lifted full of expectations and hope, until I received a second letter. The letter contained very disappointing information. After a more extensive background check, they found that the length of my American citizenship and residency did not add up to the required nine years and three months.

As a diplomat, I wanted to employ the foreign relations skills

I had practiced in Germany and Japan, and be in a position to promote social unification. I understood the regulation, but I would not accept the rejection and just give up. Instead of victimizing myself with pity, I reacted by sending my own letter to request alternative options.

To my surprise, I received a prompt reply to my letter. If I chose to accept, they would offer me a National Defense Fellowship, which would help me continue my education at a university of my choice. I knew this was a great opportunity for me, and I would not pass on such a great scholarship.

I decided on the University of Pittsburgh, the school recommended in the letter for its graduate program in International Relations, as the place to earn my masters.

Before I could enroll at the University of Pittsburgh, I needed four additional credits to finish my undergraduate studies, so I chose an English class to improve my language and communication skills. I took a class for credit, and even decided to audit another class.

A few days after classes had begun the student sitting in front of me caught my eye. She kept her attention focused on the professor, so I never saw her face, but I could tell she was well-mannered and proper. At the end of class I watched her get out of her seat. A little shorter than average, with large, but gentle eyes that softened her appearance...she intrigued me.

In the hallways, she showed a warm smile and a generous heart, giving me the courage to approach her. Before I saw her, I considered American girls a little frivolous, and had no interest in starting a relationship. Especially being in my last semester with my future secured, I was absolutely content with my life. I didn't need to complicate my situation.

But one day, I overheard her speaking with a classmate about Pittsburgh, and I seized the opportunity.

"Do you know Pittsburgh well?"

"As a matter of fact, I do. But why do you ask?"

"I need to know about the area. Do you think you could help me?"

"I'm from Pittsburgh."

We were brought together by fate.

"My name's Paull, by the way."

"I'm Donna."

After explaining my situation, I succeeded in acquiring her phone number, but it took some convincing to make her accept my dinner invitation.

We went to a nearby Chinese restaurant, and talked so much that we needed our food reheated. Aware of my time constriction, I spent as much time with Donna as possible.

For our second official "date", Donna accompanied me as my partner at a picnic. I noticed that Donna always wore long skirts, even on the day of the picnic, so I asked, "Don't you think pants might have been more comfortable for this occasion?"

"Well, my mom prefers that I wear skirts, because she still believes pants are unladylike."

Coming across an obedient woman in such a liberal country surprised me.

Our picnic included a hiking excursion, which meant more discomfort for Donna. I felt sorry for her inconvenience, but I enjoyed offering my hand for support. My feelings for Donna did not compare to all my past attempts at love. She possessed the ability to captivate my heart just by her presence, but never tried to take advantage or manipulate my feelings. Her beauty remained vivid in my mind at the end of each day, but I looked forward to refreshing my memory at any given time. I felt a strong conviction of my growing love for her, and I needed to find a way to let her know.

I was running out of time, but I didn't know how to approach such a delicate subject with a woman I could not bear to lose. I feared my impulsiveness would chase her away. Every day, I waited for an opportunity that refused to come. On our third date, we dined at a nice restaurant and went into the city to watch the big-screen version of <u>West Side Story</u>. Watching the lovers in the film defeat opposition to protect their love encouraged me to take a risk. I parked my car in front of her apartment, and hesitated to say good night. Instead, I started to stutter a confession.

"Uh Donna…I think I'm in love with you."

I still don't know what possessed me to start out so bluntly. I just didn't know how to decorate my thoughts, but Donna surprised me more with what she said next:

"Does that mean you want to marry me?"

Her boldness made me completely forget my own train of thought, so she continued, while I fumbled for words.

"I've considered marriage…"

I couldn't decide if she accepted or declined my proposal. She had already anticipated my intentions even before I built up enough courage to do anything about it, so did that mean she had already made up her mind?

"Marriage is a very serious commitment. Do you think you can wait for me?"

I took her answer as a gentle rejection. In order to protect my feelings, I refused to contact her or try to change her mind. To my surprise, I received a call from Donna, on the following Sunday afternoon, asking me to meet her. I needed to calm my frantic heart before meeting Donna, so I opened up a map, and found the nearest cemetery. I remembered sleeping in the cemetery as a young boy when I wanted peace and comfort—both of which I needed desperately.

We drove to the cemetery in an awkward silence. I'm sure neither could offer small talk or conversation, but the silence was disturbing.

I stopped my car in front of the cemetery.

"Why did you bring us here?"

"I find the cemetery comforting and safe. If it's okay with you, I'd like to talk here."

"How strange."

She seemed a little uneasy, but she found a spot in the grass and settled down. Donna broke the silence.

"I thought about your proposal, and I don't see anything to hinder us from getting married, because I feel you're the one for me. There's just one stipulation. We must have my parents' blessing."

"How could we win their approval?"

"Why don't we try calling?"

We called her parents in Pittsburgh from a public phone near the cemetery.

"Hi Mom, it's me, Donna..."

They continued with small talk.

"Wow, what's the occasion?"

"Can you guess why I called?"

"Well, that's not fair."

"I uh...Mom, I found the person I want to marry."

"Really? Who is it? What's his name? How did you meet? What does he do?"

They continued with excitement as Donna's mother asked questions, and Donna tried to brag about me.

"His name's Paull Shin..."

There was a long silence.

"Shin? That means he's..."

By Donna's silence, I could tell her mother had already addressed the issue of my ethnicity.

"He's Korean," Donna explained.

When Donna's father picked up the phone, they repeated a similar conversation, except this time, Donna handed me the phone.

"Would you please tell me who you are, and why you want to marry my daughter?"

"I just finished my undergraduate studies at the university, and I'll be attending The University of Pittsburgh this fall to earn my masters. I love Donna, and I plan to love her for the rest of my life. Please consent to our marriage."

"Can you take full responsibility for my daughter's well-being and happiness?"

"I'll do the best I can."

"If you're coming to Pittsburgh, I'd like to meet you. We'll talk more then."

Without the immediate opposition from Donna's parents, I put the receiver down eagerly, but dread and concern settled in.

"This society frowns upon minority groups, especially inter-racial marriages. In fact, most states prohibit interracial marriages. Do you think your parents could allow our marriage?"

"Don't worry too much. There is more diversity where my parents live, and they know the love and laws of God."

"How can I make a good impression on your parents?"

"I'm warning you now that my mom will be more difficult, and she likes someone with a tidy appearance."

When I was young, I wore whatever I picked up, until the army gave me a uniform. In America, I wore what I was given, and after I became independent, I bought clothes from second hand stores and the Salvation Army to conserve money. For the first time in my life, I spent a fortune on a three-piece suit, and risked a heart attack just to impress Donna's mother. I loaded all my belongings into my Volkswagen, said my final goodbyes, and headed towards Pittsburgh.

living with my in-laws

At the end of three long days of driving, a sign welcoming me to Pittsburgh appeared. I followed an address to my host family the school provided. On the second day, I put on my new suit to look my best, and went to the church that Donna's parents attended for Sunday worship.

Inside the church, a familiar looking man walked towards me to shake my hand. I recognized him from pictures as Donna's father. We exchanged conventional greetings, but an awkward silence immediately followed. Luckily, it was time for the main worship service to begin, so we walked into the chapel. Donna's perky, teen-age sister, Gloria eased the tone with her excitement. When I didn't see Donna's mother even after the service started, I quietly asked Gloria where her mother was. Gloria uneasily moved aside to reveal her mother. Donna's mother had been sitting next to us without making her presence known to me. I extended a polite greeting, but she barely acknowledged my effort.

I didn't find her attitude encouraging, but I understood her reasons. I searched throughout the whole sanctuary, but I stood out as the exclusive Asian, and I seemed to be the center of attention.

Discrimination never repeats identical emotions, nor can I anticipate the disguise it takes. Even a church harbored room for prejudice, but I wanted to dismiss the attention as curiosity.

As we walked out of church, Donna's father spoke first.

"Why don't you join us for dinner?"

Gloria jumped at the invitation, and volunteered to accompany me in my car. Her optimistic attitude helped me forget my troubles temporarily, but as soon as we arrived at the two-story, brick house, my misery returned. At the door, Donna's mother examined my appearance, and walked in without voicing her opinion. The suit was worth every penny!

During the meal, Donna's father directed the conversation.

"What will you do after you earn your masters?"

"I'm hoping to become a diplomat."

"About your marriage to my daughter…we're going to need some time to think it over."

"I understand your concern. I'm prepared to wait."

In a way, I wished I could get a straight answer and lift the burden, but I knew that I needed the time to prove myself to Donna's parents.

Although I lived with a host family near the University, I met

Donna's parents at church every week, and joined them for dinner almost every Sunday after church.

All the neighbors noticed my frequent visits to the Skaggs family home, but remained polite. While the neighbors tiptoed around the subject, Donna's mother boldly replied, "I'm against the marriage. Even the law prohibits interracial marriages. How would they survive the racism?"

Once they heard this, they spoke freely of their own opposition. Donna's mother was very hard to impress in every aspect, but she applied the same rigid standards on herself as well. She was a perfectionist who didn't even appear before her children without makeup.

Donna and I spoke on the phone once a month at an appointed time, but wrote letters everyday. I never questioned Donna's faithfulness, but I worried about other men who might assume her availability.

The rest of Donna's family accepted me more willingly, which drove Donna's mother to desperation. Seeking some advice and hopefully support, Donna's mother wrote a letter to a leader in the church, stating her daughter's intention to marry a Korean, her own disapproval, and premonitions for the future.

She received a reply that strengthened her opposition, and reaffirmed her determination to separate us.

Despite the lack of theological justification to disapprove of a union between couples from different ethnic backgrounds, there were many reasons for the church leader's reservations. Aside from the legal barrier reflecting the prejudices in our society, he also identified issues concerning the future of our family, and the problems our children would face. The church leader advised against the marriage because of the obvious repercussions.

This letter provided all the reinforcement she needed. Donna's mother showed it to anyone who approached the subject, and used it as reference for any disagreements in the family.

As Christmas approached, I began to anticipate my reunion with Donna. Her train stopped by Chicago, so I took a train out to meet her, and escorted her through the remaining distance. We used the hours to make up for all the time we missed, and shared exciting stories narrated in our letters. Even with the elapsed time, I only had enough courage to hold her hand, and otherwise kept my distance, especially in the presence of her family.

I came to the house every morning to spend the day with Donna—always under the scrutinizing glare of her mother.

In an impulsive attempt to persuade her daughter to think realistically, Donna's mother showed Donna the letter from the church leader. As a result, however, Donna's mother's hopes of separating us vanished. Donna became more adamant and replied, "No matter what other people think, we have to remember that God loves this man. I want to stand by him, and do what I can to protect him."

At the end of winter break, Donna returned to Utah, leaving me alone, once again.

When Donna's father suffered from a heart attack, I was able to show my commitment and sincerity by volunteering myself as the chauffeur to the family. Donna's father had to stay in the hospital for a while to be monitored, but Donna's mother had never driven a car before. She could not get to and from the hospital on her own. In order to accommodate the family emergency, Donna's father suggested that I move into the house temporarily and commute from there.

I packed my VW with my belongings once again, and moved into Donna's old room. It felt as if I could still feel Donna's presence in the room. We were so far away, yet I felt so close.

I tried to make myself invisible. After going to the bathroom, I opened a window and fanned out all the smell with a newspaper so that no one would suspect what I had done. Donna's mother spent most of her time in the hospital, but I was responsible for transporting her there. Spending so much time together allowed us to feel better acquainted, but not quite comfortable yet.

At the end of one week, Donna's father returned from the hospital, and I chose to move back to my host family. I imposed too great of a burden on Donna's mother for me to stay very long.

I continued my Sunday afternoon visits, and then early in May, I heard Donna's father calling me, "Paull, my son! Can you come here for a minute?"

Son? Did that mean he's decided to allow the marriage? I probably heard wrong...and even if he did say it, I'm reading too deeply into a simple endearment.

When I rushed to hear what he had to say, he proudly stated, "You now have my blessing to marry my daughter. Many states have yet to legalize interracial marriages, and human prejudices will make your life difficult. Love each other, support one another, and more than anything, be understanding. Then no one can break the union God has formed."

I was so touched by his approval and acceptance of me as his son-in-law, even despite knowing that our marriage was illegal in most states. His blessing meant more to me than any of the social pressures against us.

I wondered what Donna's mother had to say about his decision, but at this point, I had no objections. After calling Donna, my father-in-law-to-be called the rest of the family to tell them the good news.

"Donna graduates in three months and you'll be out of school for the summer. Why don't we arrange the wedding to take place then?"

After that day, Donna's mother started to soften up to my presence, even giving me a smile every once in a while. Despite our differences, she never failed in her obligations. She was always courteous in her treatment towards me, and lived each day with the same dedication as the previous. I think we even shared an alliance as a family.

Donna and I lived with her parents for a while after our marriage, and when my father-in-law passed away, I invited my mother-in-law to live with us. She lived with us for about 18 years until she herself passed on, but for those 18 years, she always provided kimchi on my table, and welcomed the endless flow of guests entering our home. She never tried to deny or justify her disapproval at the beginning of Donna's and my relationship, but once she changed her mind, I was constantly reminded of her support. Race had created an invisible wall within the family, but we learned to accept each other with love.

Since the matriarch lived with us, our home became the headquarters for all six of Donna's siblings, and we felt responsible for everyone's welfare.

On my mother-in-law's 70th birthday, we invited about 100 guests and held a three-day long party. As a gift, we presented an opal ring with a diamond embedded in it. When she received the present, she threw her arms around me and exclaimed, "Paull, you're my favorite son-in-law!"

uncompromising happiness

Many superstitious Koreans believe that a June bride lives in happiness. What more could I ask for?

My in-laws took a train to Utah, and I drove my car out. I had been anticipating this event for a really long time, and made many sacrifices, but with the fruit of my efforts within reach, I feared the consequences to follow.

"Donna will face rejection to stand by me, my children will suffer for their differences…I know I can't protect them from society…is my happiness worth the pain of so many others? How can I qualify as an acceptable husband and father?"

All the horrors of my imagination kept me awake while I drove nonstop for two days. When I arrived at my parent's house, they welcomed me home. The condition of my mother's health did not allow her to travel the distance to attend the wedding, but we spent the evening discussing issues of marriage, family life, raising children, etc. Who better to receive advice from than an exceptional mother and wife? She enlightened me on the mysterious ways of women and revealed to me as many secrets as possible to help me understand my future wife.

Before I left, they congratulated me, wished me all the best of luck, and my father slipped a check in my pocket as a wedding contribution.

I arrived at Donna's apartment to unload some things, and as I got out of my car, Donna ran out and kissed me. Too surprised to enjoy it, I just turned red with embarrassment. All my worries and doubts vanished like the morning mist with a glimpse of Donna's innocence.

The next day, we drove to California, where interracial marriages were allowed. After ten hours of driving, we arrived at Donna's older sister's home, and dropped off our luggage. When we went to the Los Angeles District Court to receive a marriage license, I learned an astonishing fact. I had assumed Donna to be well in her twenties, but skipping a grade in elementary school and another year in junior high left her at nineteen, nine years younger than me. I felt like I was committing a crime or violating some unspoken rule.

Overwhelmed with shock and disbelief, I ended up spilling the milkshake in my hands all over Donna's new dress, and my new suit.

"After tonight, I'm going to have a family of my own, in a society where racism seems acceptable, even customary. How will

My bride, Donna
So innocent and pure.
Next to my wife, I looked uncomfortable and nervous.
People say a couple grows to look alike,
but I think Donna and I have conserved our differences
throughout the years,
growing closer with understanding.

I console my family, and help them overlook the insecurities I feel? Whom can we rely on for support and encouragement?"

On June 12, 1963, we held a very humble wedding for those congratulating our union. Even our speaker seemed to insinuate his concern.

"America is a truly blessed land, but far from perfect. Exercise patience, and develop an understanding, but trust in God, and turn to Him for healing."

Throughout the whole ceremony, I kept my attention focused on surviving the procedures without revealing my cowardice. I regret that I never studied Donna's reactions, and her expressions, because when I look back on our wedding day, I only remember my own feelings of fear and inadequacy, and how nervous I felt.

The rest of our family and friends waited for us at the reception. Even my father sent a gift through another relative, with a letter of encouragement and support. After receiving all the congratulatory remarks, Donna and I drove away from the people shouting encouragements, towards northern California, and the rest of our lives.

We planned to spend our first night in Santa Barbara, but it was only 7 p.m. when we arrived, and still daylight outside. At the front desk of the motel, our eyes met and I lost the courage to ask for a room.

"Why don't we go a little further?"

Neither of us hesitated to jump back in the car to continue our journey. I kept driving until I was too tired to go any further. I took an exit to a small town called Buellton, and looked at my watch to find it was past midnight.

"We haven't even eaten dinner yet!"

After checking into a motel, we went across the street to a well-known diner called Anderson's Split Pea Soup. By the time we returned to our room, it was past 2 a.m. That night, we fell asleep to the pounding of our hearts.

Early the next morning, we started north on U.S. 101 towards Carmel, our honeymoon destination. We made all the tourist stops along the way, from the historical Spanish Missions to the small fishing village. When we drove by admirable mansions, I silently vowed to buy Donna the kind of house she deserved one day.

Throughout the honeymoon, our appearance attracted curiosity, and provoked discrimination wherever we went. I wondered what they disapproved of the most. Me, the American women associating with an Asian, or anticipating the possibility of more couples like us... Nevertheless, we refused to allow their opinions to compromise our happiness. Rather than subjecting ourselves to the negativity, we concentrated on preserving our own experience of love.

We did a lot of window-shopping, and walked along the beach barefoot to feel the cool sand tickle our toes, and let the water wash away the rest. We even dined in some fine restaurants, but on the third day, we turned toward Utah. Without very much money, Utah was our only refuge. In order to travel a two-day distance in one, we avoided any unnecessary stops. I drove the whole time while Donna tried to keep me awake. She talked, she sang, and when all else failed, she even pinched me. A feeling of reassurance accompanied the pain of each pinch as I absorbed the reality of her company.

"I'm not alone anymore."

only the beginning

Donna returned to school as soon as we arrived in Utah, and I found a job to fulfill my responsibility as the sole provider of a family. Thinking of the possibility of children in the future motivated me to work harder. Donna had to finish some credits to graduate, and I returned to the elevator company, where I knew a job always waited.

It was during my summer vacation in 1961, after completing a day of toil in the sun when I happened to peek into the building of an elevator company, where they held a special lecture. I asked one of the employees if I could listen, but he hesitated to reply. I quickly offered to clean the office in exchange for the lecture. From then on, I stopped by once in a while to listen to lectures, and cleaned in return. When the president of the company heard of my arrangement, he asked, "Where do you work now?"

"On a construction site," I answered.

"Why don't you work here in this company instead?"

I gladly accepted the job. What an honor to work indoors! The backbreaking labor earned me $1.95 an hour, but I would receive $2.50 an hour for working as an elevator technician's assistant. What a stroke of luck!

One day, the technician decided to stop working just because his workday was over, but I stayed behind to complete the job we had started. I preferred to spend an extra 20 minutes to finish the work while the elevator was set up, rather than wasting an additional hour to re-setup the elevator the next morning. As I continued to work, the president happened to walk by and saw me working.

A few days later, we received our paychecks, and the president called me aside.

"Paull, I saw you working overtime a few days ago, but why didn't you request overtime compensation?"

"Oh, I was just eliminating some extra work for the next day. It hardly counts as overtime."

"You know what? I want to hire you as a permanent employee. If you ever need a job, remember there will always be a job here waiting for you."

I thanked him for the offer, and took advantage of it whenever I had a few months to make extra money even after I got married, and because of my experience in Utah, I got a job installing elevators in Seattle during my summer vacation and winter holidays while I was attending the University of Washington for my doctorate.

Donna and I spent the first three months of our marriage completely satisfied with each other's company. But summer break always seems to end too soon, and before we knew it, we had to load up the Volkswagen and drive back to Pittsburgh to complete my master's degree. As I parted with my father, an unexplained sense of grief swept over our hearts. Looking back, 40 years later, I think I must have felt some sort of premonition letting me know I was leaving Utah for good this time. Till this day, I have not been able to return to Utah, for anything more than short visits.

Since Donna and I cut our honeymoon short, due to lack of time and money, we spent our trip back to Pittsburgh as a second honeymoon. We traveled through famous tourist attractions, and enjoyed the natural environment. Up until the moment we reached Donna's parents' home, we were determined to live on our own in Pittsburgh, but as soon as Donna's parents started to plead with us, we easily fell to their persuasion.

During a trip to Chicago for a series of Peace Corp training lectures at the Northern Illinois University, we encountered some racist bullies in front of our hotel, just itching with boredom.

They looked young, but they outnumbered me seven to one. I faced a losing battle, and even if I won, I knew I would end up severely injured. So I bluffed a little, imitating a semi-martial arts position, and confidently approached their weakest link. He slowly inched away, and eventually turned around to flee. The rest of the group quickly followed.

As we rejoiced in our victory, an unspoken shadow darkened our hearts. How long and how often can I keep up my phony bluffs? Even more importantly, how will our relationship survive the animosity and danger?

once a be**gg**ar... now a profe**SS**or

Upon receiving my Masters, I was appointed to the BYU Hawaii campus as an assistant proffessor.

From the Honolulu airport, we drove about an hour and a half along the coast to reach the university, which looked more like a beach resort than a university campus. The waves crashing against the shores electrified our excitement as Donna and I followed directions to our own two-bedroom faculty house.

Compared to my homeless life in Korea, and all the years of careful avoidance, a house reserved just for Donna and I felt like enclosed freedom. The previous owner left me a bicycle to use as a mode of transportation, so I rode the bike on my first commute to school.

Donna escorted me outside, and continued to wave until I rode beyond her horizon. I felt uncomfortable leaving Donna by herself all day, so I kept looking back.

The agreeable autumn weather seemed to forecast the rest of my time in Hawaii, and I welcomed the promising future.

On my bookshelf, all the books I ordered as required texts, and some other supplementary reference materials waited for me in a neat stack. I looked outside my window to see students carrying books, and without warning, my heart started racing.

"Even after ten years in America, my English still faltered. Why would my students trust me with their education?"

I prayed, "Father, grant me your wisdom, lend me your strength. Help me to lead these students in the right path."

My first priority was to teach the students everything I knew, to the best of my abilities. If there was a student struggling the way I did, I promised myself to help them with everything in my power.

I taught East Asian history, and world civilization. I reviewed, and thoroughly researched each lesson to eliminate any mistakes, but my hands trembled with anticipation everyday as I opened the door to the lecture hall. Before I knew it, I was already preparing for lesson 14 in my World Civilizations class.

"Please open your books to chapter 14."

"Chapter 15," someone cried out.

I usually prepared one lesson in advance, so it would have been easy to adjust if I had made a mistake. But when I double-checked, I saw that we had only completed the first half of chapter 14.

"I see why you might think so, but since chapter 14 is divided into two sections, we're still studying chapter 14."

"Chapter 15!" he said it louder than the first time.

I looked around to match the voice to a face, and found that he was a well-built guy who looked half Polynesian and half white. The easiest solution was to ignore his interruption.

"Let's start with the second half of chapter 14."

"Chapter 15!"

I couldn't disregard the situation any longer. The other students would think I was afraid of confrontation.

I took my time walking towards him and said, "You are interrupting my class. If you cannot cooperate, please leave."

"Who do you think you are telling me to leave?"

Now he was challenging my authority.

"I'm obligated to provide a positive learning environment to the rest of these students, and you are disrupting this lesson. Please leave right away."

He hesitated a little bit, but in the end, he gave in to my command, grabbed his belongings, and stormed out. On my bike ride home that day, I couldn't even enjoy the scenery. Kicking a student out of my class made me question my priorities, and my ability to control my emotions.

I spent a restless night, but in the morning I found that I had lost sleep over a problem waiting to provide its own solution. When I walked into my office, the student was waiting for me.

He nervously said, "Professor Shin, I want to apologize for my behavior yesterday. I promise not to disrespect you like that again. Please forgive me."

What a relief!!!

"I think I might have been too hard on you also."

We parted on good terms, and remained that way.

His name was Leonard Beck, who happened to be a Polynesian hula dancer. He invited Donna and me to visit the Polynesian Cultural Center, where he worked, and introduced us to the native culture. I still meet him every once in a while on a screen, because he found a position in Hollywood.

After the Beck incident, I faced my students with more confidence. The Asian students started to respect me as a mentor, so the school appointed me as the international students' advisor. It opened opportunities for me to travel on recruiting missions to different Asian countries.

When Donna became a junior high school teacher, we decided to put her salary in savings for future use, and used mine to take care of bills and other living expenses. We sent a third of the remaining amount to my father in Korea to help the family, so despite the increased income, we lived on a strictly limited budget.

Life seemed pleasant until Donna, who was usually healthy, started to feel dizzy, and weak. She had such a hard time waking up in the mornings and couldn't eat, so we went to the hospital. When the doctor congratulated us for a pregnancy, both of us started to bubble in our own excitement. I would catch myself laughing for no reason at all, and noticed the questioning glares, but ignored them. The pregnancy, however, ended in a miscarriage despite the extra precautions.

"God will give us a healthy baby next time. I'm just glad

you're still healthy."

We consoled each other, and looked forward to hearing good news again.

As the number of Korean students increased, so did my responsibilities. I had students coming in and out of my office, seeking more than just academic advice, and became involved with the students' personal lives. Finding jobs, housing, even significant others. I played a successful matchmaker to a few couples, and witnessed their marriages.

In any situation, I always made an effort to include the students who usually segregated themselves from the rest of the group. I felt the importance of building a community for minority groups—a place to feel accepted usually helped build confidence and self-esteem.

Even though I played the aggressor in the social lives of others, I avoided conversations with strangers because of lingering insecurities. At the second Christmas party for Korean students, a graduate student from the University of Hawaii approached me, looking a little drunk.

"Which university did you go to in Korea?" he asked.

He was making an attempt to be sociable. I hesitated to answer his question, but he stood waiting for a reply, so I stuttered in Korean, "I didn't go to school in Korea."

"Ignorant bastard! Why are you even here then?"

This insensitive student had no right to chastise me for my ignorance. Humiliated and furious, it took all my self-control to refrain from throwing a hard punch at the student. I definitely couldn't defend myself in a heated debate, so I walked out on the party to cool off, and started walking. What started as a superficial conversation turned into another emotional battle with my insecurities.

In the freedom of solitude, I cried aloud. All my hidden complexes started to re-emerge. Who selected me to live an unfortunate childhood? By now, I had surrendered to racial discrimination, but realizing that I was still vulnerable to persecution from my own kind cut me deeper than any slandering remarks.

That evening, I drove twenty-seven miles, from Honolulu to my home in Laie in a reckless mess of tears and anger. I stopped several times to rage about the injustice and pity of my grievances. By the time I arrived at our house, five hours later, I had come to one resolution: "I'm learning Korean whatever it takes!" When Donna opened the door, I saw the relief wash over her worried face.

I started to ask my students simple grammatical questions, and began a painful attempt to relearn Korean. For a while, I never let go of my contempt towards the student who revived all my terrors of ignorance. I wanted to hunt him down and teach him to think again before insulting someone the way he insulted me. I still wish to see him again. However, I have no intention of fighting or seeking revenge. I only need a few minutes to thank him. He opened my eyes to an unavoidable obstacle, and caused enough rage to fuel my determination. I needed to learn Korean.

To this day, I never explained to Donna what happened that night, or where I spent the five hours.

Sharing a Dream

returning to the Motherland

As the international students' advisor, one of my assignments was traveling to Asian countries to recruit students, and promote the university. In the summer of 1965, Donna came with me, and we also visited Korea. I didn't want to reveal my past to her. I didn't want her to see the poverty and deprivation that shaped my childhood, but as my wife, she deserved to know. In order to understand me, she needed to see. I also wanted to pay long overdue visits to my biological families.

After visiting Manila, Hong Kong and Taiwan, we arrived at the Gimpo International Airport in Seoul, Korea. A reporter noticed that I was traveling with a white lady and stopped me to ask a few questions at the gate.

"What brings you to Korea, and how long has it been since you last visited?"

"It's been eleven years, and I'm here to interview students."

"Are there any significant changes you see here?"

"I see many more smiles."

The reporter asked me a few more questions before leaving, and a couple days later, the headline of a newspaper read, "A street rat returns eleven years later as a successful professor, with an American wife, and a new perspective on life. He sees more smiles on the faces of those around him. Perhaps the difference is a change in his own attitude."

From the view in my taxi, the streets of Seoul seemed unchanged, but I still felt disorientated. Donna preferred to rest in the hotel, so I headed towards Namdaemun (South Gate) Market alone. The layout of the allies and back corners of my childhood habitat remained the same, despite the new buildings. The streets may have looked the same, but they definitely felt different under my feet. I used to walk around barefoot, but this time my feet were covered with socks and shoes.

Once I entered the Market, I noticed that everything seemed more crowded than before, but it was still the same merchandise and food. In their struggle to survive, the ladies selling food and other products must have grown bolder, because they yelled much louder and persuaded buyers much more aggressively.

I remembered stealing fruits and vegetables from carts. The sting of an owner's slap across my face still remained as if I had made the unsuccessful attempt to steal food just yesterday. As I finished a hot bowl of noodles in a corner store, I temporarily forgot that I was a grown man, and walked out with tears streaming down my face. My appetite must have changed as I grew older, because the noodles seemed to have lost the magical taste I remembered. Feeling disappointed, I found my way to the Seoul Train Station: the source of many nightmares, my escape from the cold, my shelter from the rain, and a home when all else failed. I could almost feel the warmth I shared with Jaewon, my childhood friend, as we relied on each other to avoid freezing to death.

It only took one look to refresh my memory. With the exception of an increase in population, everything else remained the way I remembered. I weaved through the crowd and was stopped by a young boy with his dirty hands extended to the crowd. I placed some money in his begging hands and quickly turned around to hide the tears gathering in my eyes.

I had finally returned.

Jaewon, can you see me? I've come back as a college professor. I have a beautiful wife too. What else can I do to keep my promise to you? Am I living a life enough for two?

Reminiscing painful memories allowed me to reflect upon my blessings and successes.

The next day, Donna and I took a bus to Geumchon. While we waited, and even on the bus, Donna experienced the discomfort of curiosity and prejudice I fought in America. I realized it hurt more to see Donna as the victim, than when I dealt with the pain for myself.

The bus ride seemed unusually bumpy along the gravel road. I don't even know how we managed to stay in our seats. As we approached the vicinity of my grandmother's home, I trembled with growing anticipation. "Am I too late? Has my grandmother passed away?" I pushed open the picket fence, and faced my aunt.

"Hobom? Is it really you? Mother! Hobom's here!!! He's returned!"

"...Mother?" That means she's alive!

"What? What did you just say?"

A door flew open, and my grandmother tumbled out wide-eyed, and of course, barefoot. She could barely tilt her neck far enough to see me, because her back hunched even closer to the ground.

"*Aigo*, you're alive! You've returned! If this is a dream, don't wake me up just yet."

We cried in each other's arms and shared an emotional reunion.

"Grandma, this is my wife."

She looked up to discover the foreign woman. Donna politely bowed her head and my aunt spoke first.

"Wow. She's really beautiful!"

"You mean to tell me she's my granddaughter-in-law? She looks like a human doll!"

My cousins peered out with curiosity, and my grandmother quickly introduced us.

"Don't just stand there. Say hello to your cousin, Hobom and his American wife."

"Only if your mother could see you now...she'd be so proud...poor thing..."

Once the initial excitement subsided, my grandmother started to explore and examine Donna's features. She took advantage of Donna's presence and thoroughly enjoyed her first encounter with a white woman.

My aunt scraped some food together and set a dinner table for us. The villagers invited themselves into the home once they heard of my return. The younger women admired Donna's clothing, and the older women marveled at her skin and the texture of her hair. Donna never looked bothered or annoyed. She must have felt uncomfortable, but she seemed to have surrendered herself as an educational artifact.

"Have you seen your father?"

"Not yet."

"You must go see him first thing tomorrow morning."

I followed my aunt's directions to my father's house in Yeongdeungpo. I always approached a reunion with my father full of fear and anxiety. I still carried unresolved issues of abandonment, and unable to predict my father's reception, I remained absorbed in my own thoughts for the majority of the trip.

"Hello? Father, it's me, Hobom."

My father threw open the door to confirm what he had just heard, but he remained frozen and completely speechless. My stepmother and siblings staggered out first but stopped in their tracks again. Even after I introduced Donna, nobody moved.

The tension started to loosen as my stepmother came to her senses and led us inside. Shy but curious, my younger siblings huddled among themselves and whispered to each other. As soon as I unleashed the gifts, their discomfort vanished with the wrappings. My father expressed his emotions with a few welcoming words, and resumed his silence. Despite his detached reactions, my stepmother's excitement showed me that my father had worried about me.

I wanted to show Donna all the tourist attractions, many of which were also unfamiliar to me. Already accustomed to the gravel roads, we enjoyed our bumpy bus ride from Seoul to Nonsan, a central part of South Korea.

Since there were no hotels in such a small city at the time, we went to a nearby inn to check in but when the owner saw us, he said, "Sorry, we don't have any rooms available."

"What do you mean? Why not?"

"Actually, we don't have any beds."

When the owner saw the "American" woman, he assumed that we needed a bed. I explained to him that a bed was unnecessary, and asked for a room. Once our bags had been taken care of, Donna and I went out to explore the region. The main purpose of the trip was to see the bronze, meditating Maitreya Buddha, one of the seven national treasures built in the seventh century during the Baekje Dynasty. He represented the practice of self-examination through meditation, to achieve reincarnation.

When we returned to the inn, a bed waited in our room. It was completely unexpected, and I asked the owners, "Where did this bed come from?"

"Our village mayor happened to have one in storage, so I

borrowed it from him," they replied.

We genuinely thanked him for his thoughtfulness and consideration.

The next day we continued our journey south through Gwangju and Mokpo. From Mokpo, we took a tugboat to Busan. As our boat slowly approached the Busan harbor, I felt like entering a mother's embrace. I spit in this harbor full of contempt and revulsion, but over the years, I developed a yearning for the land that gave me life.

All the contempt from my past started to overwhelm me, but Donna held my hand and quietly said, "This is your homeland, your motherland. Please accept it in your heart." Unlike the harbor, I knew my own image had taken a new identity. It was time to put away the bitterness and shame.

Donna and I stayed in Busan for a day and traveled north through the other side of the peninsula. In Gyeongju, the imperial city of the Shilla Dynasty (57 B.C. to A.D. 935), we witnessed the precision and diligence of my ancestors through the intricate details and elaborate decorations. Early the next morning, we rushed past the stone-carved image of Buddha in the Seokguram grotto, and watched the sun rise over a neighboring mountain. We held hands as we watched the beautiful sight. It seemed the sun rose for the sole purpose of brightening our day.

Back in Seoul, I searched for my friend Woonsub in the Catholic Church, only to discover that he was no longer working there.

We continued with our journey to Japan to see some of my

old friends. During one of our meetings, we must have eaten contaminated sushi, which forced us to stay in bed for two days. After two days, Donna and I started to feel better, and immediately craved Korean food again. We went to the Ginza Strip and found a Korean restaurant.

The female owner looked surprised to see Donna enjoying all the spicy foods. She came to our table to say, "Thank you for enjoying Korean food," and took off the gold necklace she was wearing to give to Donna. She also gave Donna a Korean cookbook, written in English.

Using the cookbook as reference, Donna cooked meals for the Korean students in Hawaii. Their appetites showed us how much they missed Korean food, and gave Donna a boost of confidence in her cooking abilities.

"They must have liked what I made. They ate all of it!" Donna exclaimed joyfully.

The cookbook came in really handy throughout the years. Whenever we had Korean guests coming over, Donna easily looked up recipes, and provided delicious meals.

Our trip to Korea helped me overcome a lot of anxieties about my past and reshape the image of my roots. I remembered my promise to Jaewon a long time ago: a promise to live a life fulfilling enough for two people. My journey through life was far from over, but I was not ashamed to face Jaewon's memory.

reclaiming my **i**dentity

What started as a two-year commitment in Hawaii turned to three, and it was time to move on. I accepted the job in Hawaii to build experience and determine whether or not I wanted to continue teaching. But the closer I got to my students, and the more recognition I received, the more inadequate I felt.

As our ship sailed away from the harbor, all my treasured memories of Hawaii became a distant fantasy of another life. I lingered on deck until the land of palm trees completely disappeared from my sight, and promised myself to return after I received my doctorate.

The ship we rode was a cruise ship that started in 1927, departing from San Francisco, to Hawaii, through Japan, the Philippines, Malaysia, Hong Kong, and returning to San Francisco. The captains boasted that the cruise ship had continued operation through major wars and economic crises. This was supposed to be our vacation, but even on the ship, I looked for something to do.

From Hawaii to Asia, I gave lectures on Asian history and culture to the American tourists visiting Asian countries, and as we picked up students planning to study abroad in America, I gave them thorough orientations on the basic requirements for international students studying in America. Bored with the same environment, audiences looked forward to my lectures, while Donna and I enjoyed a free, month-long vacation on a luxurious cruise ship.

I remembered the foreign exchange students standing awkwardly during school events, unable to sing an unfamiliar American National anthem. Luckily, there was a music professor also on vacation, so at my request, she agreed to teach the American National Anthem to the Asian students. Within the hour, the students sang the anthem confidently, while the music professor and I congratulated each other for the great accomplishment.

"Now that you've mastered the American anthem, why don't you share your own national anthems?" the professor asked the Asian students.

The, Japanese, Filipino, Malaysian, and Indonesian students all took turns singing their anthems but the Chinese students, making up over 50% of the students present, just sat there, nervously looking at each other. Only then did I realize their dilemma. There were three different categories of Chinese students represented. The majority were students from mainland China, who were refugees escaping Communism, and refused to sing the Communist anthem. As a British colony, Hong Kong taught "God Bless the Queen" and Taiwan, arbitrarily categorized with China, sang the Chinese Nationalist anthem brought into Taiwan by leader, Chiang Kai-Shek and Chinese Nationalists. No one volunteered to represent China, Hong Kong, or Taiwan, and the audience grew impatient. The music professor finally shouted, "Let's hear the Chinese anthem!"

Feeling the pressure of obligation, a few Taiwanese students came forward and started to sing their own anthem from Taiwan in tears. That day, the Chinese students showed me the detriment of division within a nation, and the tears of the Taiwanese students helped me reflect upon the importance of having the rights of autonomy.

I witnessed the separation of friends and families because of the ideological differences that still keep Korea divided between the North and the South, so I understood the agony of unwarranted pain, and the hesitation to sing a national anthem reiterated the value of unity.

Even if the ship provided all the extravagant luxuries, entertainment, and social events to anyone's satisfaction, once someone spotted dry land, everyone swarmed with exhilaration. Dry land symbolized freedom, hope and refuge for anyone held captive by the ocean. When the captain announced our nearing arrival in the San Francisco harbor, I was immediately transported to the time I first entered the Golden Gate. In any circumstance, the harbor never failed to amaze me.

Starting with my first view of the magical harbor, I evaluated the race I had been running to that point. I couldn't remember a time when I stopped for a break, or even a deep breath. I only had myself to use as a standard of competition, but in the process, I realized I had never established an identity to call my own.

We rented a Mercury station wagon, loaded everything we owned, and drove through Oregon to reach Seattle, a land occupied by mountains and lakes, and a city neighboring the ocean. Seattle was where I first set foot on American soil, and now I returned to complete my doctorate at the University of Washington.

When I decided to study for a doctorate, I considered many factors before deciding on a school. I always had the option of returning to the University of Pittsburgh, but I wanted to go to a school with a stronger Asian Studies department, so I applied to five different schools known for an advanced Asian Studies department: Columbia, Harvard, Michigan, Stanford, and the University of Washington.

I received acceptance to all five. Harvard and the University of Michigan even offered me research assistant positions, Stanford gave me a teaching assistant fellowship and the University of Washington even offered me a scholarship. With all the prestigious esteem associated with Harvard, I naturally wanted to go there. However, after much consideration, I decided to study at the University of Washington where there was an independent Korean Studies department.

I was drawn to the hope of reclaiming my identity and overcoming my inferiority complex toward the culture I needed to embrace. The convenience of the location also played a great role in choosing Washington. Donna's mother lived in Montana, and I wanted to stay in a quieter city, comfortable for Donna, and safer for the children we planned to have.

Donna found a job as a junior high school teacher, and as soon as I adjusted to my schedule, I visited Professor Doosoo Suh, a professor of Korean language and literature.

The first thing he said to me was, "Mr. Shin, you should learn Korean language."

It was more of a command than a suggestion. I had been trying to learn Korean, but unsuccessfully, despite my aspiration, there was no structure to my attempt. Preferring to forget the Korean I spoke on the streets even stripped me of the little advantage I could have had.

I started to visit Professor Suh three times a week for a total of nine hours a week to learn Korean. The first year he taught me from *Hangul*(Korean alphabet) to grammar and pronunciation. When I thought I had learned enough, he introduced Chinese characters in respect to the Korean language to get a better understanding for context origination and definition. I was still struggling to memorize the characters by the third year when Professor Suh assigned Korean and Chinese literature and historical documents to translate. Famous folk tales like *Chunyangjeon* (equivalent of *Romeo and Juliet*) may be a beautiful performance to watch, but to translate it into English meant fully digesting all the underlying connotations and trying to capture all the subtle nuances that are impossible to translate across cultures.

At the end of the third year Professor Suh took me out of the classroom, and continued my lessons in the community. He said, "Paull, now I want you to improve your conversational Korean by serving the Korean community. Living as an outcast of the Korean social hierarchy for so long instilled fear and caution in the way I approached Koreans, but I knew it was a mountain I had to climb, a river I had to cross, and a battle I had to conquer.

My love and respect for Professor Suh developed through his devotion and commitment to educating someone like me in the practices of a culture I had once forsaken. I showed my gratitude for all of his efforts by mowing the lawn, cleaning around the house, and running simple errands. Donna and I also played the role of family in the absence of his children who lived on the East Coast, but the only way I could truly express my deep appreciation was to try my best in all the tasks he placed before me, no matter how challenging or impossible the mission.

Through Professor Suh, I met Professor Byoungik Koh, a visiting professor from Seoul National University. Professor Koh gave me another command: "Paull, you should learn about Korean history."

I didn't have any objections, so I started to learn the history and culture of Korea, which promoted pride in my image of Korea.

Barely a thousand Koreans lived in the Seattle area when I arrived in 1967, but the population steadily increased to about seven thousand. Welcoming immigrants at the airport, introducing different jobs, admitting children to school, finding housing, escorting them to immigration offices, hospitals...my duties didn't end there. Domestic problems and traffic violations required my translation in courtrooms. I visited the district courts so frequently that the clerks not only recognized me, they considered me a friend.

I helped other immigrants to fulfill an obligation as an already established citizen, and those I helped repaid me by treating me to Korean dinners. My reputation slowly spread as "Paull Shin the pig," and my Korean language continued to improve as my weight increased.

In a land of prejudice, I strived for assimilation, and tried to identify myself as an American by abandoning my ethnicity. But no matter how hard I tried, I never got further than an Asian who spoke English very well, while Koreans criticized me for being an ignorant fool who couldn't speak his own language. Ostracized by both cultures, I questioned my identity.

"Who am I?"

Through the eyes of my friends and family, I learned to love myself, and found security. With the help of other Koreans, I reclaimed Korea, and concluded a long period of confusion. Knowing the language and understanding the culture provided me with the confidence I needed to emerge into American society.

love is thicker than blood

Donna and I waited many years for children of our own, but after the first miscarriage, we never had another opportunity. Then one day Donna suggested, "Paull, why don't we adopt a child?"

"Let's wait a little longer," I replied.

Many conservative Korean men still refuse to acknowledge children outside their bloodline as their own, but my hesitation didn't come from the conformist outlook. I feared the possibility of another pregnancy after an adoption.

Being only human, I anticipated feeling partial to the child of our own blood, and didn't want our impatience to result in a mistake, but I quickly changed my mind.

"What would I be doing now if I hadn't been adopted?"

After consulting with the Washington Children's Home Society, we agreed to adopt.

That summer, we received a call while we were painting our house.

"We found the perfect child for your family. An adorable two-year-old boy!"

I immediately dropped the paintbrush in my hand, cancelled the vacation we had planned, and rushed to the foster home where our child waited.

The social worker could not even begin to express how adorable the boy was. I gently took him in my arms, and watched his huge eyes grow bigger with curiosity. The shine in his eyes seemed to resemble Donna's eyes, and I believed that we had been destined to be a family. Because of the significance of my own name, I passed my name onto him, and added Young as his middle name. I held Paull Jr. as if I had discovered a treasure.

The small child completely uprooted and transformed the whole pattern of our lives. Donna acquired a 24-hour job, and I lost all ability to focus on my work. Imagining the moment I returned home occupied my thoughts when I was away, and at home, I refused to lose a moment with my son. Our home suddenly swelled with crying and laughter.

Three months later, we received another call from the Washington Children's Home Society.

"This time, a girl has just been born."

Donna and I went to the Virginia Mason hospital, and met a baby girl whose long eyes seemed to show stronger Asian characteristics. She was so precious that I was afraid to touch her, but as soon as I held her in my arms, I felt the force of life generate from her tiny body. We named her Alisa Myong Shin, and she made perfection inadequate.

Now our home was overflowing with life. The children took turns crying or cried together, and we could barely hear each other crying for help. We couldn't walk anywhere without tripping over toys and baby supplies, making it impossible to find a seat or take a break. Donna even quit her teaching job to take care of the children. When relatives decided to join the chaos, our home exploded with life.

My parents visited us often, mostly just to spoil their grandchildren. They always brought gifts and toys for the kids and made us adults feel left out...but as a grandparent myself now, I fully understand why we were ignored.

I always kept an interest in adopted children. I wanted to provide an understanding environment for my children, and my own history as an adoptee encouraged me to seek support. I eventually became a founding member of KIDS (Korean Identity Development Society) with about 10 other adopted families in Seattle. The membership progressively grew, and grows beyond 500.

We held celebrations for Korean holidays, and organized culture camps during the summer as educational tools for children to correctly evaluate their cultural heritage. Workshops included Korean language, history, dance, Taekwondo, calligraphy, cooking, games, other forms of entertainment, and much more. Our main objective was to familiarize adoptees and their families with Korean culture.

Establishing the organization was much easier than maintaining circulation. Inconsistencies and lack of commitment from volunteers forced us to rely on the parents rather than help from the community. Thanks to those who continually support KIDS, the organization still exists today.

I didn't limit myself to KIDS. I became involved with worldwide organizations such as WACAP (World Association of Children and Parents), HOLT adoption agency, and cultural groups like the Morning Star Korean Cultural Center. I even played an active role in the personal lives of many adoptees.

In a nearby city, a family contacted me, and asked for my assistance. They had adopted a 14-year-old boy, and despite their limitless accommodations and dedication, the boy acted like a stranger.

"Dr. Shin, we would like to meet with you concerning our adopted son from Korea."

"How can I help you?"

"We adopted a fourteen-year-old boy from Korea two years ago because we really wanted to provide a home and family for him. We have been doing everything in our power to make him feel welcome, but he will not even attempt to warm up to us. What can we do?"

"I'll try and talk to him...but I can't say I know enough about him to be of any help. Does he have any special hobbies? What does he usually do after school?"

"Well he really likes basketball, and he practices with a team

Smile for the camera!
A family with such a diverse background,
united by love and the relationship of a family.

on Mondays, Wednesdays, and Fridays from 2:30 to 4:30 at the school gym."

"Okay. I'll go see him. What's his name?"

"Peter."

I wasn't a psychiatrist, but I remembered a time when I was in a similar situation and thought I could help relate to Peter by sharing my experiences. I visited him at his basketball games and practices three times a week for about a month. The first time I walked into the gym, I spotted Peter right away since he was the only Asian student. I waved at him with a big smile.

He looked at me and turned the other way. He must have assumed that I had mistaken him for someone else. I continued to visit him, but only waved and watched him play until the end of the third week when Peter finally returned my greeting with, "Why do you keep waving at me?"

So I casually answered, "Well, I thought I could wave at you because we kind of look alike."

It took a while for him to start waving back, but I continued with regular visits. I wanted to earn his trust before prying into his life. It took almost another month before he agreed to have ice cream with me.

"Why are you so interested in me?"

"Peter, I think we could have a lot in common. I too was adopted when I was sixteen. Do you like your new home?"

Before he answered, he looked down, and tears poured out of his eyes. Then he said, "I don't feel like I'm accepted by them. If they adopted me, why don't they treat me like their own son?"

"What do you mean by that Peter?"

"All my life, I wanted to become a part of a family, so I came here full of expectations. But they treat me like a hotel guest, not a son or a brother. They have two other children of their own, who are only seven and eleven, but they have chores like doing the dishes, cleaning their room, and even some yard work. If they misbehave, they get punished and spanked. I don't have any chores around the house, and I never get spanked. Am I their son or just a hotel guest?"

I shared Peter's shocking response with his parents and continued to visit Peter for about another month until one day he ran towards me as a completely different person. He ran to me waving his arms in the air, and exclaimed, "Dr. Shin, Dr. Shin! Guess what?"

"Whoa, calm down! What happened, Peter?"

"My dad spanked me last night! Puahaha! Now I know I'm their son, and I know they really love me! I finally feel like I've become a part of the family!"

Peter went on to graduate from a university and now serves as an officer in the United States Army. Despite his initial dilemmas and uncertainty, Peter grew up to be a respectful adult, a proud American citizen, and a happy Korean adoptee.

Raising children demanded patience, and a willingness to love unconditionally.

Having acquired a love for music, we bought two pianos, hoping our children could become pianists some day. I suppose my own deprivation had something to do with it. I quickly learned that my dream wasn't necessarily theirs', and no matter how hard I tried, I failed to enforce my own desires on my children.

Even if they fell short of my expectations in some areas, they were still my children, and I loved them no less. I may have even spoiled them a bit.

When the kids were in grade schools, we bought them a Pekinese dog, and named her Pecky. Paull and Lisa really loved the dog, but unfortunately, Pecky fell victim to a tragic car accident. The driver felt terrible, but what could he do? I offered to replace the dog, but the kids said it would be much too painful, and they wanted to remain loyal to Pecky. Too bad my children were extremely devoted to their dog, because they insisted we take her to the vet. Again, I offered a replacement, but they refused. I figured listening to their request was the fastest and easiest way of alleviating the pain, so we took poor Pecky to the vet.

The vet must've had very advanced tools, because he claimed the dog still had a heartbeat. He also implied that through surgery, the dog had a chance of survival, but the odds were very slim. We allowed our children to persuade us into authorizing a $2,000 surgery that miraculously saved Pecky's life.

Pecky lived six more years as a one-eyed cripple, walking around side-ways like a drunken sailor.

The blood flowing through our body is vital for individual survival, but in determining family or friendship values, bloodlines hardly guarantee a successful relationship.

After the Korean War, a solution to the war orphans and abandoned children in an impoverished land came in the form of adoption. Many American soldiers remembered the homeless children, and adopted individually. They also made referrals to friends and family, which created a greater demand for Korean children. Missionaries established more structured organizations to reach a greater variety of adopting families. HOLT Adoption Agency, the Lutheran Childcare Service, and the Catholic Children's Service provided many homes for Korean orphans first in the United States, and then all around the Western world such as England, Sweden, Switzerland, Germany, Australia, Canada, France, Norway, Holland and Australia.

Some people oppose inter-racial adoption because it causes many identity issues as the children grow older. I can't deny its existence because I know a story of an adoptee who left "Who am I?" in her suicide note, and killed herself. I've seen many confused adoptees, failing to find a balance between their native and adopted cultures. Some even end up in jail.

My most concrete evidence of struggle lies within myself.

I am an adoptee.

Since I was adopted at age sixteen, a year after the Korean War began I'm most likely the oldest Korean adoptee in the world. With a mother whose face I don't even remember, and a father better described as a distant acquaintance, the emergence of my adopted father, mother, and three brothers introduced me to a relationship of love and happiness.

Korea actually closed the door to inter-racial adoption for a while. Not for the concern of the children, but as a way of showing the world that Korea was no longer the basket case situation of the Korean War aftermath. Orphans were considered a domestic problem that should remain within the country and no longer required the charity of others.

What Korean administrators did not understand was that parents adopted Korean children for the improvement of their own family, and not solely from altruistic motivations. Adoption eventually reopened when they realized that Koreans rarely adopted out of bloodlines, and the number of orphans kept growing out of hand.

Now there are many conferences and organizations geared towards adoptees and their families, to help them understand and even value their native country. The Korean government also extends efforts to welcome adopted families back to Korea. Organizations like the Overseas Korean Foundation or KAAN (Korean American Adoptee Network) coordinate annual conferences, and provide an environment of sharing and learning. I try to attend as many of these events as possible, partly because I also benefit from hearing and contributing insights on different issues surrounding adoption, but my main incentive to participate is the joy and privilege of building relationships with people. We talk, we laugh, and through these rather casual interactions, we help each other in our struggles with identity. Running into adoptees who suffer from personal conflicts discourage me, but I also have to keep in mind that nine out ten adoptions remain successful.

I volunteered many times as a chaperone for adopted children coming to America from Korea to meet their adopted parents, and watched many families unite with love and affection. I also became the father of adoptees, and the problems we encountered cannot be considered exclusive to adopted families.

The love we share surpasses all the boundaries of blood.

I acknowledge the significance of the old Korean saying, "Blood is thicker than water," but I learned a much more important lesson: "Love is thicker than blood."

The adopted father and his adopted children
Blood is thicker than water. But love is thicker than blood.
My adopted parents and my adopted children gathered in one place.

dear st**a**rs

Dear stars…

I'm sure you know,
The thoughts of pessimism and negativity,
Spreading…
To disappoint and despair.

I'm sure you've heard,
The words of conspiracy and contempt,
Speaking…
To injure and scar.

I'm sure you've seen,
The actions of tyranny and oppression,
Dominating…
To deprive and repress.

I'm sure you've felt,
The hearts of jealousy and envy,
Reaching out…
To divide and disperse.

if sand could tUrn into concrete…

Koreans are often referred to as sand. Each grain portrays the distinct, adamant characteristics of Koreans. Mixing water into the sand helps create majestic castles, but the crash of a wave obliterates the sculpture, wiping away any evidence of its existence, and destroying the unity required in creation.

I offered my services to the Korean community as a donation of my personal experiences and knowledge, but as my popularity increased, so did my obligations. A husband, a father, a son, a brother, a student, a professor…in order to prioritize my life and keep some sense of balance, I needed to eliminate unnecessary commitments, which entailed severing my ties with the Korean community, but I never learned to ignore another's plea for help. The Washington State Korean Association President of 1974 appointed me as his Public Relations Officer, and I couldn't refuse the position.

At the end of the year, the officers prepared to choose the next president as they always had. Unlike previous years, however, we faced some opposition.

"Why should officers hold all the presidential power? You must open the position to the public, and give everyone an equal opportunity."

In the past, instead of holding complicated elections, we chose presidents by agreeing on an appropriate nominee, which also promoted more of a family atmosphere. As the Korean population expanded, however, our methods grew increasingly ineffective, and the community demanded a more structured and formal election.

Determined to gain control of the Korean Association, the opposing party recruited a busload of voters from a neighboring city, while our side made no such arrangements. Allowing the elections to proceed without an opportunity to campaign meant handing over the presidency without an attempt to protect it, so we postponed the election. Once both sides had an equal opportunity to campaign, the community was completely divided. In this endless game of tug of war, the opposing sides finally stepped aside and agreed on a third delegate—me.

I never expected the nomination, and was even less prepared to accept it. My Korean still broken, my ideologies still foreign, but for the sake of unity, I inherited my appointment with humility, and resolved to try my best.

As president, I wanted to change the focus of the Korean

Association from a social gathering to a service organization. I also wanted to extend our networks beyond the Korean families, into all the diverse communities in the area. I believed that through cultural exchange, we could take advantage of ethnic diversity. The council members worked hard to come up with tangible goals, and to promote the various activities. Executing our reforms required additional sacrifices and unexpected obstacles, but the results compensated all our efforts. Even Donna contributed her services by preparing meals for the meetings and guests in our home.

We accepted the paper work for foreign exchange students, immigration documents, interpretation, and any other ways to volunteer as the responsibility of community leaders. I created English language classes for the first generation immigrants, and Korean language classes for the second generation and adopted children. In an effort to provide more connections to the mother-land, we hosted festivals and celebrations for various Korean and American National Holidays: Independence Movement Day (March 1), Liberation Day (August 15), commemorating the Korean War (June 25), a day to celebrate the 4th of July and Christmas. All this also helped to give Korea greater exposure and representation. We even worked to build a Korean Community Center. In order to start construction, we needed to build financial security, so we participated in every opportunity to raise money. We sold Korean food at different festivals, and when Halloween season came around, we put aside our dignity to sell pumpkins on the streets.

In 1975, as another outreach project, we hosted a Korea Day Banquet. We invited the governor, government officials, business and community leaders, schoolteachers, Korean War veterans, and the parents of Korean adoptees. Approximately five hundred people joined in the festivities that night at the Four Seasons Hotel, and gave us the opportunity to publicly express our appreciation for all the benefits offered by America. We wanted to thank those present for allowing immigration, employment and business opportunities, excellent education for our children, adopting and loving children from Korea, and even fighting for Korea in a time of crisis. As long as we were living together, we wanted to promote better relations among the diverse communities. We may have met as strangers, but now we can improve our relationship as friends and partners, working to create a better environment.

Eight years later, with another election coming up, I was called to join an emergency meeting. About forty members of the community gathered to discuss, and hopefully find a solution to a very grave political situation.

"Dr. Shin, the Korean Association and the Korean Consulate need someone to step in as a mediator. You're the only one with enough influence to reinstate the peace in this community. We asked you to come here, hoping that you'll agree to run for president."

"I already served a year in '75. There's nothing more I can do."

"If the opposing side should gain presidential power, we'll spend the whole year in dispute between the Korean Association and the Korean government, which puts the interest of the community last."

Those who opposed the so-called President Chun, Doohan's dictatorship in Korea decided to reject all government dispatched officials, including the Consulate General, by deporting them out of Seattle. They chose someone who led the protest against the Korean government to run as the president.

I resisted their persuasion till three in the morning, but a single voice could not compete with the relentless demand of a community. With less than two weeks till the election, we actively campaigned, and struggled to campaign with integrity.

On a very snowy election day, we remembered the shrewd tactic of the opposing party in the election eight years ago, and imported a busload of Koreans from a neighboring city. Even with the additional reinforcement, we won by a very narrow margin of only 28 votes. With instability in the Korean government, and suspicion among us, I predicted a very difficult year. The Korean Consulate, and my supporters breathed a sigh of relief, but I stumbled with the burden of achieving unity and peace.

Our problems started sooner than we expected. As soon as the election was over, the opposing team sued us for dishonest vote count and causing a disruption of peace in the community. The judge dismissed the case for lack of evidence, and when the opposition returned for an appeal, the judge laughed, and asked us not to involve the court in such domestic problems.

My greatest obstacle lie in the hearts of those refusing to acknowledge my presidency as a legitimate appointment, but I needed to look past their defiance and find ways to contribute to the community while gaining their trust and cooperation.

The Korean population in Washington State had more than doubled over the years, so I expanded the already established Korean language classes, and improved the programs. We took another step into the multi-cultural society by participating in the annual Sea Fair Torchlight Parade. In the presence of over 350,000 live spectators and an even larger television audience, we shared the excitement and beauty of Korean culture. At the time, there were no groups or organizations in Seattle capable of performing for such an important event, so we recruited volunteers and taught them basic rhythmic patterns, but also invited special guests from Los Angeles to raise the quality of our performance. The process was not exactly painless, but once the parade began, all the frustrations of preparing disappeared and left me with pride in the cultural excellence of Korea. Sounds of the gongs and drums reverberated throughout the streets of Seattle and the audience showed their appreciation with encouraging shouts: "Thank you, thank you for sharing your culture with us."

In the following years, I continued to support the Korean Association, and actively took part in various organizations. Accommodating the demands of a multiplying population of Koreans occupied a large portion of my time, but I gladly volunteered my services to the community. Working so closely with my Korean associates increased my own personal awareness of identity, and helped me overcome a lot of childhood insecurities.

Because of the manipulation, exploitation, and antagonism of some, I encountered the optimism, assistance, and encouragement of others. A crashing wave may disrupt the community, but Koreans' dedication to a movement or demonstration also ignores previous hostilities, to produce amazing results.

Now only if…some secret ingredient of concrete could be added to the sand…just imagine the possibilities!

a professor and a business**m**an

As planned, once I received my doctorate, we packed our bags, sold the house, and prepared to return to Hawaii until we were hit by the realization that we now had our children's future to consider. We remembered the lack of opportunities in the Hawaiian Islands, and hesitated to raise our children in such a vacation oriented society.

Through prayer and careful evaluation, Donna and I agreed to settle down in Seattle. Since we already sold the house we owned, we bought a new home, which has remained our permanent residence for over thirty years.

I wanted to stay as a professor at the University of Washington and continue my academic career teaching and publishing books, but my responsibilities as a husband and father prevented me from acting selfishly especially since Donna had to quit her job for the children. Shoreline Community College offered me a full-time position as a professor in the Asian Studies Department. I gratefully accepted and even extended my teaching hours to the evening classes in order to keep up with my responsibilities to family.

In addition, the demands for financial assistance for my father and my siblings in Korea were also increasing. I continued to send some money to Korea every month for my stepbrothers' and stepsister's education, but once I realized that my father used the money on alcohol rather than anything productive, I decided to bring my siblings to America. One obstacle remained. I could barely support my wife and children on a teacher's salary, not to mention my outstanding student loans. How could I take responsibility for my siblings? How much do I need to support all five of my siblings? How can I make enough money? I needed to find an alternative occupation without abandoning my dream.

During the summer of 1972, on my way home from school one day, I noticed a sign that read, "Hiring Real Estate Agents" and in smaller print, "Training available for beginners." I stopped my car, and three months later, I received my Real Estate license. As an agent, I had flexible hours, and I could grade papers or prepare lectures while waiting for phone calls in my office.

All the advantages of a realtor corresponded to my prerequisites, but when I sat down to calculate the time I spent completing the tedious paper work, or answering the demands of my clients, I realized that the job was more time consuming than profitable.

In order to maximize my profit, I added developer to my job

description. I bought old, deteriorating homes, and remodeled them to sell with some profit. I don't even know if the extra profit was worth all the work. After school, I worked late into the night every day, including weekends. A little bit of paint and a few nails did wonders to improve the appearance of the house, but I didn't even have time to feel fatigue.

After building enough experience with homes, I moved onto apartments, expanding and renovating them to attract tenants to the previously uninviting homes.

With the money I made from my endeavors, I built credit with the banks, and they approved enough loans for me to build a motel, and buy other real estate investments. Expanding my business ventures as an investor not only provided a steady income for my family, but I could also afford to bring all five of my half-siblings, my biological father and my stepmother to America. I even paid off my college loans, which took a huge load off my shoulders.

If my profession as a businessman ended with personal wealth, I would not have been able to fully enjoy the income. I found community service opportunities as a realtor. From 1973-1975, Boeing laid off a third of its employees due to economic hardship. Since the Boeing headquarter was stationed in Seattle, one-third amounted to a lot of unemployed people.

Unable to pay their bills, so many people started to leave the Seattle area that the motto for the city became, "Last one to leave Seattle can turn off the lights." The Federal Housing Authority repossessed many homes and sold them back to low-income families at affordable rates, with no down payment. I proudly played the agent for many poor students and immigrant families. Since the commission was only 1.2%, I can't claim to have made much profit, but I felt a greater sense of satisfaction in helping poor students and their families to acquire their own homes.

In 1983, when I was re-elected as the Washington State Korean Association President, I abandoned my label as a realtor. I wanted to avoid rumors and accusations claiming that I abused my position to advertise my business, and I didn't want to compete with the growing number of Korean real estate agents. Above all, I wanted the extra time for my family and teaching.

At about the same time, I received a call from Coldwell Banker, a commercial real estate corporation and the biggest real estate company in the United States. The company offered me a position as a board member. I was very interested in such an attractive offer from a nationally growing company. In a management position there was no inventory, so no risk of loss?only possibility of great wealth in the profit sharing. They extended me an offer to pay what was three times my current salary, plus bonuses and stock options, and I could help them tap into the rapidly growing Asian market. I had no reason to turn down such a mutually beneficial opportunity. However, there was one stipulation.

"Can I continue teaching while working for you?" I asked.

There was a moment of silence, then loud laughter.

The representative from the firm said, "I'm sorry, you'd be in a full-time position, and so I'm afraid you would not be able to keep the teaching position. I am offering you an opportunity to become a very rich man, and you want to continue teaching?"

If my childhood dream had been to become a rich man, I would have accepted the position without hesitation, and have become a multi-millionaire by now. However, I dreamt of becoming a teacher, and I treasured the value of education. I declined the offer, and pursued my dream as an educator.

Due to inexperience, I made many regrettable choices, lost money, or established businesses that caused more trouble than produce revenue. My biggest mistake was to trust a dishonest stockbroker who lost an extremely large sum of money. Looking back, however, I realize that despite my oversights and miscalculations, everything worked out for the best, and allowed me to live within my own means.

I opened investment opportunities for my extended family, found jobs for the unemployed, gave profit to the banks, and even made a minor contribution to the economy in the process. If I possessed no personal income, I know entering a political campaign would have been very difficult, and regaining confidence after failure might have been impossible.

My most rewarding accomplishment was having the ability to help my father when he needed an escape from financial difficulty. It all started with a phone call from my mother.

"Paull, I think your father's in some sort of financial trouble, but he refuses to tell me about it. You may want to come here and speak to him about his finances."

I decided to take a short trip to Utah, and spend some "quality time" with my father. My excuse for visiting was extremely vague, so I couldn't avoid the issue for long.

"Dad, I can tell something is bothering you. Can you tell me what it's about? I want to help you if I can."

The words sounded familiar to me, except this time, I was the one probing in hopes to be of some assistance. Luckily, my father did not resist my offer or try to keep his problem from me.

One of his students had come to him with an idea of inventing a personal computer. He needed to build a prototype, and materializing his idea cost a large sum of cash. This student had a PhD in mathematics, and my father saw his potential, so he borrowed a large sum of money from the bank with his own credit. Two small prototype PC's were produced with the money, but three weeks prior to receiving a patent, IBM marketed almost identical personal computers.

IBM's claim to personal computers invalidated all the money and effort put into building the prototypes, but my father was still responsible for repaying the loan, with interest.

I couldn't deny my obligation, and fervent desire to help my father, but I wasn't sure how. During my time as a real estate agent, I developed an eye for evaluating land, and as I drove around that day, I spotted a perfect site for something.

Considering my parents' age and future, I concluded that a nursing home would be most appropriate, and went to work. I contacted the Department of Health and Social Services for an industrial revenue bond. The Hill Haven Nursing Home Management Company, stationed in Tacoma, Washington, agreed to manage the nursing home, and I received government guarantee for a public project loan, with a lower interest rate.

We completed a 120-unit nursing home, and paid off my father's debt by May 2, 1986. For the building dedication, we invited the mayor, government officials, health care representatives, and the general public. In the presence of approximately 200 guests, my father said in tears,

"Many people advised me against bringing Paull to America as my adopted son, but I was determined to keep my promise to a young boy. Now that boy has grown up to thank me in a way I never imagined. He willingly accepted my burden as his own, and discovered a solution."

He then took my hands and continued to say, "I never expected anything or dreamed that you could help me like this. When I first held these hands in Korea, they were blistered by the wind, filthy with dirt, and exhausted from rejection, but these hands delivered me from financial depression, and these hands helped me stand up. I feel that even if I die now I have no regrets."

I'm not, by any standards, a financially secured man, but I make sure I pay my tithing and offerings to the church, give regular donations to charity funds, educational and cultural advancement programs, adoption organizations, and many more outreach associations. Out of respect for elders, I always supported numerous senior citizens' organizations, but I realize that now, as a fellow senior citizen, I'm entitled to take advantage of the contributions I've made.

A very modest sign expanded my occupational grounds to

unexpected domains, but I reaped much more than I had sown. How did such an inconspicuous sign catch my attention? If I learned anything, it was to never dismiss minor, insignificant details, and I re-examined the value of seizing every opportunity placed before me.

reunited with my biological family

I learned to speak proper Korean from Professor Doosoo Suh at the University of Washington, but he made an assumption that almost cost me my relationship with my first brother. He forgot to teach me one of the most fundamental rules of the Korean language—one that is universally understood within the culture, but not always explicitly taught to people born into the language. Knowing that I had grown up speaking Korean, Professor Suh never reminded me of the three linguistic variations of Korean: an informal version for referring to inferiors, a slight moderation to imply equality among friends, and honorifics to show respect for elders or connote formality.

Without formal education, I was incapable of reading and writing, and growing up on the streets of Korea, I had been mostly exposed to the crude language used by street kids and gangsters, and speaking to my relatives had not required much knowledge of subtle linguistic distinctions. From Professor Suh I learned what I lacked. I learned how to speak respectful Korean. What I didn't realize was that it was the wrong Korean to use with friends and younger brothers and sisters.

After I had established some financial stability, I invited my younger brothers and sister to join me in America. Kilbom, the oldest of my five younger siblings, came first. I went to the airport to pick him up, but I realized that I had not seen enough of him to spot him out of a crowd at an international gate. He recognized me first, and started to walk in my direction. I initiated the conversation by saying in my very best Korean,

"Excuse me sir, are you Mr. Kilbom Shin?"

He looked startled, and it took him a moment to respond.

"Huh? Yes!"

"Welcome to America, sir. I'm really glad you could come here, sir."

Now he seemed really confused. I assumed that long hours on a plane and the unfamiliar environment disoriented him.

We decided that Kilbom needed to learn English first, so I enrolled him in an ESL class at Seattle Central Community College.

Before we had a chance to get better acquainted, Kilbom moved into an apartment closer to school. We met regularly throughout the week, and he stayed at our house on the weekends, but an invisible barrier lie between us. I hoped time would help break down the wall, and I waited for Kilbom to feel more comfortable with me. One day, a drunk and thoroughly irritated Kilbom confronted me.

"*Hyungnim* (older brother)! I need to speak with you."

"What is it, sir?"

"I left everything behind and came into this foreign land with no one to trust but you. See! Here I am, but you still keep your distance!"

"What do you mean, sir?"

"What do *I*…?"

Seeing that I was genuinely confused, he stopped to look at me.

"You're my older brother, but you speak to me in that respectful tone!"

"I'm sorry sir, but is there something wrong with that?"

"Yes! You're talking to me as if I was your elder, or a stranger. Why don't you drop the honorifics and treat me like a younger brother?"

That night, Kilbom gave me a very important lesson on the Korean language. Once he realized how ignorant I was of the social nuances of Korean, his anger disappeared, and we laughed together at my ignorance.

Even after clarifying our misunderstanding, communication between the two of us seemed strained. I had become fairly fluent in functional Korean when it was directed toward a specific purpose, but casual conversation felt like a whole new language to me. I talked to Kilbom every night, but I always struggled for things to say. In the end, I would revert to the conversation from the previous night.

"Hi, it's me."

"Hi, Hyung."

"How was your business today?"

"Fine."

"Did you eat dinner?"

"Yes."

"Why don't you go to sleep then?"

We repeated the same dialogue everyday, until one day, Kilbom asked me, "Hyung, don't you have anything else to say to me? I'm getting tired of answering the same questions!"

When Kilbom was ready to start his own business, I helped him purchase and run a mom and pop convenience store in Seattle. I agreed to help Kilbom under one condition: that he stops drinking. I attributed most of our family's problems to my father's alcoholism, and I shuddered at the thought that Kilbom might follow his example.

Late one night, I stopped by his store unannounced, and interrupted a drinking party. Disappointed and furious, I turned to walk out, but Kilbom's friends rushed out to explain.

"It's not his fault! Please forgive him! We forced him into this."

I pretended to give in with great reluctance, but I actually had no intention of turning my back on Kilbom.

"Okay, I'll forgive you this time, but if I ever catch you again, you know the consequence!"

Kilbom respected my decision, but the extremely popular,

Reunited with the family I left behind
Related by blood but practically strangers by acquaintance
only. the years would bring us closer together as a family.

twenty-six-year-old could not escape peer pressure for long. One day when I visited Kilbom's store, I found him trying to resolve a conflict with an older Korean couple.

"Don't ever call our house again!" the man yelled at Kilbom.

"What happened?" I asked the man. "Did my brother do something to offend you?"

"It's bad enough calling so late at night, but he doesn't even have the decency to be courteous, let alone apologize! He was rude, impolite, and extremely disrespectful to my daughter-in-law. She was so upset she couldn't even defend herself!"

Unable to understand what had happened, and sensing that I needed to get Kilbom's side of the story before getting further involved in the incident, I apologized to the couple, promising that whatever happened would never happen again, and sent them home.

As soon as they were gone, Kilbom told me the story. He and his friends had been at a party. When the man's son didn't show up, Kilbom, at his friends' insistence, called his house. His wife answered and said her husband was asleep.

"I didn't believe her," Kilbom told me. "And I was a little drunk. I guess I insulted her, but I didn't mean to. It's my fault, I know. I'll accept any punishment you give me. I'll go back to Korea if you want me to."

Although I was disappointed with Kilbom for breaking his promise to me, I also felt that the father had overreacted. He was caught in the trap of an angry father, fed up with his own son's disobedience. My brother was paying for the bad behavior of the whole group. I decided that Kilbom had already received enough punishment, but we needed to repair relations with the other family. The next day I took Kilbom to his friend's family to make a formal apology.

With flowers in hand, we humbly entered the home, and I kneeled before the couple to apologize. In many ways, it was a potentially humiliating situation for me, but it served the purpose of not only earning the family's forgiveness, but also strengthening Kilbom's resolve to stop drinking.

Today, Kilbom is a great husband, a loving father, and a loyal brother—an exemplary man all around.

Two years after Kilbom came to the U.S., my third brother, Inbom, and my youngest sister, Chansoon, joined us in Seattle. My experience with Kilbom helped me with Inbom. I adjusted to him right away, and we didn't experience any of the awkwardness or misunderstandings that had troubled my relationship with Kilbom. Chansoon was in junior high when she came, so I felt more like a father than a brother.

Over the next ten years, I would bring the rest of my Korean siblings to the United States. The last of my family to arrive would be my father and his wife. Their arrival marked the end of my long struggle to forgive and accept my father. It took so long because I always harbored resentment towards him for abandoning me at the age of four.

In 1976, I went to Korea to unite the gravesites of my grandfather, grandmother, and mother into one family plot in my home town of Geumchon. My father, who had remained indifferent even when I bought him a house in his hometown of Pajoo, seemed genuinely grateful. He had been living in a rented shack next to a textile factory, and I wanted him to have a home he could call his own. I know he appreciated my concern, but he never displayed his emotions. I thought my father set the standard for the detached, unemotional Korean father.

"I should've done this a long time ago," he said. "Thank you for fulfilling my responsibilities."

With these words from my father, the "inexpressive Korean father" became a myth.

Nevertheless, things didn't really change between us. Despite my respectful attitude toward him, I always felt indignation flare up in some corner of my heart. I understood his sorrow, and honored him as a parent, but I could never justify his abandonment. His initial desertion left a scar that his return could not heal.

I wanted to confront him about it, but I wanted to speak to him when he was not under the influence of alcohol and at least capable of a coherent conversation.

I never seemed to be able to anticipate when he would be sober, but I learned why. I asked my stepmother if there was any way to regulate his drinking, and she told me that when my father knew I was visiting, he made sure that he was drunk before I arrived. He didn't have the courage to face me sober.

Finally, in 1989, I showed up at my father's house unexpectedly. He was not only sober, but even obliging. We enjoyed a warm and delightful dinner, which encouraged me to take advantage of the opportunity.

"Father, I have a question to ask you. It has been a burden upon my heart for over fifty years, and I don't want to feel disturbed by the past any longer."

"What is it?"

"After my mother died, how could you orphan a four-year-old boy? Why did you abandon me and where did you go?"

It took a while for my father to absorb the question, and I waited silently. When the tension became unbearable, he bolted for the door. But I was determined to wait until I received a straight answer, so I stubbornly waited for him to return.

I waited in silence until he returned at about four o'clock in the morning, filling the room with the smell of alcohol. My stepmother left the room to give us some time alone, and my father started to speak.

"How could I abandon my own child?" He began, and breathed a long sigh.

"When your mother died, we were so poor, and I had to find some way to support us. No home would hire a male servant with a child too young to help with the work, so out of desperation, I left you under your grandmother's care. Hobom, I know I don't deserve it, but please forgive me."

I bowed my head in shame as he continued.

"I even went to a Japanese labor camp to try and make a living. As soon as I remarried, I went to your grandmother's home to take you back, but you had run away. I returned to your grandmother often to hear any news of you, but they knew nothing, and I had no way of finding you. That guilt has never left me."

As my father spoke, I reflected upon my grievance. Despite some difficulties, society now considers me an intellect, and social elite. I had certificates and plaques acknowledging my educational achievements. Strangers call me "Professor" and "Doctor" but I continued to hold onto an ignorant grudge against my father. Poverty is not a crime, yet I condemned my father for what he could not control.

"Father, please forgive me. I needed someone to blame, and you were the most convenient target. All these years…"

Upon learning the truth, all my feelings of self-pity and despair escaped, and found release in tears. My father and I overcame years of separation in a single emotional night. We held each other and cried for hours before our tears dried up.

"Father, I'm returning to America next July. I want you to pack your bags, and join me in Seattle."

By the fall, my father and stepmother were comfortably settled in an apartment in Edmonds, a northern suburb of Seattle, five minutes away from my own home.

A year before he passed away, my father visited Korea, looked around his homeland, visited relatives, and said to himself, "This is my last visit." He must have sensed the deterioration in his health. By the time doctors discovered the tumor, the cancer had spread too far and too deep in his body to attempt an effective treatment.

On his deathbed, my father held my hand, and whispered, "Hobom, I'm leaving now. I'm leaving this world of frustration and torment behind, but I leave satisfied to know that our relationship has been restored. I want to thank you for bringing our whole family together in America. This must be happiness. Now I can die in peace."

These were his last words. Only the tears that continued to flow summarized his last memories of this world. Two weeks later, he passed away at seventy-nine.

I buried him next to Henry Jackson, the respected United States Senator and presidential candidate, who represents for me the model of the public servant. I admired his aspiration to learn, his humble approach, and I felt his passionate love for humanity.

Every time I visit my father's grave, I always include a visit to Senator Jackson's in my itinerary, not only to pay my respects, but also to reflect upon my own attitude and integrity as a public servant.

Reporters often mislabel me as an orphan, but that is a grave misconception. I am an adoptee, not an orphan. I have a family—an extremely large family. In fact, I probably have one of the largest extended families. I find it kind of ironic that I had absolutely no one to turn to as a beggar, but once I achieved moderate success, relatives I didn't even know existed started to show up.

No matter how busy I become, I always leave room for family, because I consider family number one in my long list of priorities.

Even today, when we run out of conversation, or feel like a good laugh, we bring up a very old, inside joke.

"Excuse me Sir, are you Mr. Kilbom Shin?"

I play right along, and we all laugh together.

at the End of his rainbow

One morning I did something I had never done before—I cancelled my classes. An inexpressible sadness had come over me, preventing me from concentrating on anything, or even performing my routine tasks. Without knowing why, as if answering a command from my heart, I jumped in my car and drove around aimlessly. I stopped in front of the Mukilteo Beach. I wondered why I was feeling so depressed. Could it be the gloomy weather? Or were repressed emotions from my childhood returning?

Lunchtime passed by unnoticed, as I stared blankly out into the horizon. When I went home later that afternoon, I decided to exercise my negative feelings away in the swimming pool, but before I could change into my swim suit, I was startled by the unusually shrill sound of my phone ringing. An uneasy feeling swept through my body as I rushed to answer the phone.

It was my brother Howard.

"Paull, I'm sorry to tell you this. I have terrible news. Dad just passed away."

At that moment I wished my brother Howard had never called. I wanted to step back a couple of minutes and erase what my ears had just heard.

"When? Where? How?"

My heart crumbled and deteriorated to the point of disintegration. The tears started to pour out.

"Today, at eleven-thirty. He was on his way to see Paull Jr. in Idaho. He had a heart attack, and his car ran into a big rock just off the road."

That would have been ten-thirty in the morning, Seattle time, about the time I cancelled my class.

"Where's Dad now?"

"He's still in the town where the accident happened."

"Who's going to pick him up?"

"We don't know yet."

"How's Mother taking the news?"

"She fainted after hearing about Dad, and she's still unconscious."

"Then you guys stay with Mother, don't worry about Dad. I'll take him back to Utah."

I hung up the phone, and sobbed without inhibition. But I couldn't stay that way for very long. There were too many things to take care of. I called the airport, but they didn't have any flights to Idaho that day. Instead of waiting for the next plane, Donna and

I drove all night to Idaho.

Was it raining? It must have been because I just remember that it was so hard to see the whole way to Idaho. But maybe it was just the tears. If Donna had not come with me, I might have faced the same fate as my father. Donna understood my sorrow, but that night, she must have been a little ashamed to call me her husband, because I know I cried like a baby.

Mixed in with my sadness was a feeling of guilt. Father had taken to visiting my son Paull Jr. in college, because he knew I was too busy. He got into an accident doing what I should have been doing.

It was already nine in the morning when we arrived in Idaho Falls. My father's body was in the police station of a small town. I hired a funeral hearse to drive my father back to Utah, and followed behind him in my own car.

Passing by a funeral car on the road is always a little depressing, but driving behind one that carried my father for five hours tore apart my soul.

I thought back to our first encounter and my first impression of the tall man with a permanent smile across his face. I remembered his piety, his dedication to charity, and his compassion. I remembered his thirst for ice water and the satisfaction washing over his face as he enjoyed the earth-cooled liquid. I idolized him, and he never disappointed me.

He sawed, hammered, and built a medical clinic for the refugees from North Korea. He had turned his backyard into a basketball court, and welcomed all the neighborhood kids...

When I bought Korean fruit for the officers, he reached out to take the first bite. When the corporal had falsely accused me of attacking him, he came to my rescue. He searched without complaint through the dusty, littered streets of Busan for the temporary Korean Government's office headquarters just to adopt me. When I moved off the army base, I waited all week for the weekend, and waited all morning for him to arrive. But when the ocean separated us, I waited two years to run into his arms again. I relived all our experiences together, and wondered when we would meet again. In the beginning he had been my savior. Then he became my father and teacher. Finally, he had become my best-friend.

We finally crossed a long bridge of obstacles to solidify our relationship into one of interdependency, and I really looked forward to reciprocating all the love and grace he had offered in our relationship. But a brief accident shattered years of expectations. At the opening of the nursing home, he had said, "even if I die now I have no regrets…" but I never thought of his comment as a premonition of the near future. He only had two months to enjoy a life free of debt. If he had died in debt-ridden anxiety, I would have carried the guilt of failing to help my father forever.

By the time we arrived in Salt Lake City, my mother had regained consciousness, and was already thinking on my father's behalf.

"Let's not spend a lot of money on floral arrangements at the funeral," she said. "I know Father would've preferred to use the money for a more meaningful cause. Since he always loved children, I suggest we donate the money to the Children's Hospital."

We all agreed, but at the same time no one really wanted to say our final goodbyes to Father in a stark setting. However, when news of my father's death reached the Korean community in Seattle, flowers started pouring in. Friends, students, business associates, Korean community organizations, the Consul General, among many others sent their condolences. Even the Korean ambassador in Washington D. C. and the Foreign Minister in Seoul sent flowers. The flowers completely filled the chapel.

Guests couldn't help but express their amazement at the elaborate decorations.

"Wow there are more flowers here than at the florist!"

I might disagree with many Korean ideals and principles, but their loyalty and sense of friendship filled me with pride.

After the funeral service, the family lawyer asked us to join him in a room.

"I'd like to read Dr. Paull's will at this time."

We all waited uneasily. What thoughts would Father reveal now? I even felt a hint of fear.

The will was very simple. Father left the house and car to Mother, and divided all of the remaining assets equally among his four sons.

The lawyer asked, "Does anybody object to any of this?"

I spoke up immediately.

"I would like to return my portion of the inheritance to Mother. I am already eternally grateful to my adopted family— Father, Mother, and my three brothers—for your willingness to adopt and accept me. From the very first time Father hugged me, to the time I finally arrived in America, I longed to be a part of a loving family such as this one. These blessings are plenty, and I do not expect anything more. When the time comes, my brothers can obtain my share from Mother."

As I kneeled before my father's grave, I remembered the emptiness I felt in Korea when I watched his jeep disappear into a cloud of dust the day he returned to America without me. I felt the same desolation now beside his grave.

I will have to wait until we meet again, in a place of no more parting, no more sadness, no more tears. For the time being, I wanted to cherish the memories in my heart.

for You, i'll be...

For your discouraged soul,
Exhausted with loneliness,
I'll be...
A radiant star at your windowsill,
Revealing new hopes, encouraging new dreams.

For your tears,
Running aimlessly down your cheeks,
I'll be...
A humble breath of reassurance,
Brushing away your sorrow in a silent whisper.

For your desolate horizon,
Saturated in agony,
I'll be...
A sympathizing robin up above,
Resonating a joyous melody across the skies.

For your vision,

Searching blindly through the night,

I'll be…

A lavish rose in full bloom,

Opening your eyes to a blossom of smiles.

one thing led to another

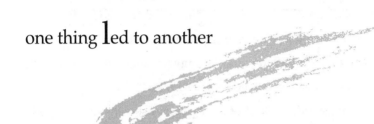

After the 1975 collapse of the U.S. supported regimes in Vietnam, Laos, and Cambodia, the United States admitted thousands of Southeast Asian refugees to the United States. Many came to the Seattle area, attracted to its temperate climate, long history of Asian immigration, and expanding economy.

In light of the ever increasing immigrant population, the Washington State legislature and Governor Daniel Evans, passed a bill to establish the Commission on Asian Americans and Pacific Islanders to assist in the resettlement of newcomers, and also to address issues of institutional, social and racial discrimination within the State. Representatives from seven Asian communities were invited, and I was appointed the representative for the Korean community. When I arrived at the capital building, I noticed that I was the only first generation immigrant in the room.

Others were all descendants of second, third and even fourth generation immigrants.

The main topic of the meeting concerned the use of a six-million-dollar grant that the State had received from the federal government to aid the refugees from Vietnam. The general consensus seemed to agree with dividing the money among the refugees. To everyone's astonishment, I opposed the idea.

I suggested, "Instead of giving them fish, why don't we help them learn how to catch fish for themselves?"

"What do you mean?" someone asked.

"Are you referring to some sort of biblical allusion?" another wondered.

"Six million dollars is a lot of money," I said, "but when it's divided, it only amounts to a couple thousand dollars per person. Within two to three months, that money will disappear. What do they do then? Who will help them next? Let's use the money to build a vocational program and give them the tools to earn their own living."

Working together, we established a vocational program that taught welding, plumbing, and shipbuilding—skills that were in great demand in the Seattle area, at a time when Boeing was building more planes, and Todd and Lockheed shipbuilding companies had a long list of contracts to fulfill.

While the program was designed with Southeast Asian refugees in mind, it was open to the general public. Hundreds of Asians, including Korean immigrants took advantage of this opportunity to increase their personal income. Graduates were able to find entry-level jobs paying between nine and thirteen dollars per hour, which was a great increase from the average five dollars an hour working in hotels and restaurants.

Economic development in Asia, and the opening of China, home to one quarter of the world's population, stirred great excitement in Washington State. As a Pacific Rim state with a growing Asian population, Washington was uniquely positioned to take advantage of Asia's growth. When Governor Dan Evans' administration asked me to help promote trade between Washington State and Asian countries, I proudly accepted the opportunity to serve my country and my state by putting my background and knowledge of Asia to practical use.

Over the course of the next fifteen years, I would serve three governors as an unofficial advisor for international trade with the Pacific Rim countries. The experience would enable me to not only contribute in a small way to trade in my state but to exchange views and concerns with many American and Asian officials and politicians.

In 1987, in the airplane on our way back from a trade mission to Asia, Governor Booth Gardner surprised me with a question.

"Paull, have you ever considered becoming a politician?"

"Who, me?"

"Over the years you've helped us so much as an advisor and interpreter. I think it's time you run for state legislature and become a leader. I've seen many sides of you—a scholar, a businessman, even a diplomat. We need someone of your caliber to help us in international affairs. I will help you get elected."

Ever since the night I was thrown out of "The Whites Only" restaurant in Texas some thirty years before, I had been looking for ways to go in the direction of a public servant, but when I faced the decisive moment of opportunity, all I could do was point to my face and ask,

"With this color? You know my district consists of predominantly white voters. No, I don't think so. Maybe in the next generation."

Years of personal struggles with my identity had weakened my determination and courage. I couldn't imagine people actually voting for someone of my color. And I wasn't sure I wanted to give up a reliable life for something as temperamental as politics.

But the Governor didn't give up. He invited me to his mansion for a "discussion", but I knew he wanted another chance to change my mind. When I arrived, two other potential candidates were already waiting.

"The reason I've called the three of you here is to ask a favor. I would like you to run for a position in the State Legislature as democrats."

The other two accepted, but I hesitated.

"Asia is progressing rapidly, and Washington needs a representative with knowledge of Asian cultures," the Governor told me. "And more importantly, as you know all too well, the Asian population in our own state is also growing rapidly."

Even with all the persuasion, my answer remained the same: "I can't."

Beyond reason or incentive, I was just too scared. I couldn't see past the impossibilities derived by my own prejudices. I questioned my ability to convince the citizens to vote for me as their representative.

My friend in Korea, Congressman Hyunuk Kim, who happened to agree with Governor Gardner, embarked on a personal campaign to convince me otherwise.

"Paull, you have to set a precedent for future generations. Your example will give them the courage to enter politics."

Nothing could prevent the doubt and wariness from pouring in. I remained unconvinced. How could I, a member of the "minority," run a successful campaign against mainstream America? I couldn't hide my identity from the eyes of society. Above all, I was adopted—abandoned by those who should have loved me the most. Even if I had come to understand intellectually the conditions of my father's abandonment, years of low self-esteem weighed heavily.

I returned to teaching.

Then, early in the winter of 1991, Ralph Munro, the Secretary of State for Washington visited me.

"Paull, I heard you'd like to join the State Legislature. Why don't you run as a Republican candidate?"

I replied again, "How do you expect me to run with a face like mine?"

"That's exactly what I'm talking about. You have a distinction the rest of us can't even imagine: You have a compelling life story. Use it to your own advantage. I'm advising you as a friend, not as a politician."

"You mean publicly expose a past I've tried to conceal and forget? Expose all the shame and humiliation?"

At first I couldn't even consider his suggestion, but the more I thought about what Ralph said, the more I began to see his point. Most Americans take for granted their lives of freedom and abundance. Perhaps my story would prompt them to reflect upon their own blessings.

I started to see some logic in his suggestion.

Around this time, Martha Choe, a second generation Korean-American ran and won a seat in the Seattle City Council.

"Dr. Shin, now it's your turn," a Korean community leader told me. "Since Martha Choe won her election, it opens the door for you."

Many people showed me their support, but they hardly spoke for the majority. I had a large coverage area, and I didn't even know where to start.

One day I happened to run into John Beck, the third-term, incumbent State Representative from my legislative district.

"Paull, the word is that you're going to run against me as a candidate for the House of Representatives. Is this true?"

"I'm thinking about it. But I haven't made up my mind. There's a lot for me to consider."

"Paull, Senator Gary Nelson from our district is running for the Snohomish County Council, and if he wins, I'll run for his place in the State Senate. So why don't you help me in this election, and when I win the Senate seat, I'll make sure I return the favor."

He was implicitly asking me not to run against him this time. Did he feel threatened by me? And did that mean I had a chance?

I felt the suggestion trigger my ambition. Maybe I had finally found a way to keep an old promise: "Someday, I will serve you." Who could have thought that fulfilling my vow would take over thirty years?

My first step was to seek the advice of many friends and colleagues. In a meeting of the Korean-American community, approximately fifty leaders unanimously agreed that I was right person to represent the interests of the community, and could serve as a role model for future politicians.

But before I could make a final decision, I had to consult with my wife not only because a decision to run was going to radically change our lives, but because I value my wife's opinion and judgment above everybody else's.

"If I only took into consideration your health and the peace of our family I would oppose the idea," Donna said. "But the minority groups and the rest of the community need you working for their best interests. As you know I am not a public person, but I will support and help you from behind if you wish to run."

In the presence of community leaders I announced my intention to run. They all voiced their support and desire to help. A campaign support committee was immediately organized.

I set a platform that emphasized the things I thought were important: education, trade with East Asia, economic growth, reduced crime, and better transportation system.

On April 15, 1992 I held a campaign kick-off party at

Edmonds Community College. In the presence of all my guests, I officially declared my candidacy for the House of Representatives in the 21st district of Washington State:

"Over the past forty years, America has constructed and facilitated a new life for me. To show my appreciation and repay some of my debt, I have decided to enter in the race for House of Representatives as a Democratic candidate. Even in my old age, I promise to try my best, and contribute all I have to offer. I was made in Korea, but recycled in America. I stand before you today with a deep desire to serve my community, state, and country, by dedicating myself to render the same great love that I continue to receive.

I hope this does not end as a personal campaign, because my decision to run stems from a desire to sacrifice myself to the community. I don't think so highly of myself that I believe other people should follow my example, but I wish to be a footstool, a step on the ladder, for others who question their ability or competence to run for political office. A dream to serve has led me this far, and my desire to serve will carry me to the end."

Governor Gardner did not end with just recruiting me as a political candidate. As he welcomed all the guests, he also publicly pledged his full support for my campaign, and asked others to do likewise.

I was encouraged by the donations collected that night and from different organizations and individuals around the region on subsequent occasions, but I trembled with fear every time I thought of the possibility of defeat. There were moments when I thought I had been crazy to embark on such a risky endeavor. The residents of the 21st district were affluent, relatively conservative, overwhelmingly White and mostly Republican. With all this under consideration, I should have chosen to run as a Republican, but looking at immigration issues, the history of human rights, support of senior citizens, educational goals among other issues, I thought the Democratic Party would be more appropriate for me.

I deserved to remain skeptical. As a third generation resident of Seattle, my opponent had deep personal and business ties with many important people in the district. He was a third-term incumbent, a former Foreign Service officer, and the owner of an essential business, Beck's Funeral Home. Most of the city's deceased lie on his cemetery. (I should know because I purchased plots from the Beck Funeral Home for my Korean father, and my mother-in-law.)

But the race had begun. "Beginning a race is as much as completing half the race," someone once said. "To quit would be more difficult than finishing."

My only option now was to keep running.

going down in history

By this time tomorrow, everything will be decided...

Election Day 1992, I trembled with doubt and questioned the odds. Would I meet the citizens in the thrill of victory or the shame of defeat?

I felt like I made an effort of a flea trying to conquer a lion. For the last 26 years, the Republican Party dominated this district. How am I supposed to overturn the precedent of such a loyal delegation? In a predominantly white district where the minority population covered less than three percent, my chances seemed nonexistent. But I had lived a life motivated by impractical hopes, and unattainable dreams...

I made every effort to play down race. Korean volunteers kept a low profile by working behind the scenes. But the uprooted and vandalized signs told us that race was a factor. Those who objected to the growing Asian population voiced their protest through their disapproval of me. Racial slurs were shouted out from passing cars or made in anonymous phone calls.

"We don't need any more Orientals around here!"

"Chink! Jap!"

"You have no business here!"

I spent the night tossing and turning, passing in and out of consciousness, until I finally decided to give up all attempts at sleep.

When I walked into my garage, campaign signs of all sizes faced me. I wondered if they would be mocking me tomorrow. I figured I should probably take advantage of them while I still had a chance, so I grabbed as many as I could, and loaded them in my trunk.

The nipping autumn wind tore through my coat, but I concentrated on displaying my sincerity towards the oncoming traffic. One by one, my volunteers joined me, and soon we were all waving signs as if our lives depended on their effectiveness. By the reactions of the drivers who honked, yelled, or showed us the victory symbol, I knew I deserved to feel a little more confident.

As the fog lifted, I noticed my opponent standing on the other side of the intersection with his supporters, waving "Re-Elect John Beck" signs. We shared an awkward greeting, and went back to promoting our names. Once the rush hour started to subside, the volunteers' fervor also dwindled and they went on to return home, or go to their own work place.

We tried to encourage each other as we parted. Everyone

guaranteed victory, but I still lacked absolute assurance. Back home, I knelt before God in my office.

"Lord, the day has finally come. I'm overwhelmed by your provision and grace. You have opened many opportunities for me, and led me this far. With gratitude and deep appreciation, I have done everything in my power for this race, and now the results lie in Your hands. You know the needs of this community, and if I fulfill Your demands, do with me as You wish. Please eliminate all selfish desires, and hopes for personal glory. I ask that Your will be displayed in all the coming events. In Your name, Amen."

Donna and I went to a nearby elementary school to exercise our rights as American citizens, and to contribute two more votes to my name.

As we were walking out a man approached me to give me the most encouraging greeting I could expect.

"Hello Paull! I just voted for you."

I returned his kindness with, "Thank you very much! I can only hope for the best."

I really hoped that every vote would make a difference.

After dropping Donna off at home, I set out again to hold up some more signs.

"You're going out again?" Donna asked.

"Of course! This is my last chance."

"I don't think it will be very effective today. Everybody's already made up their minds," Donna tried to comfort me.

"I have to try."

As I stood out on the street one last time, I was glad that after tonight, I wouldn't have to be a solicitor of votes anymore. The thought gave me relief, but also brought a sense of regret.

I returned to my office to thank my supporters before the results came in. If I failed, where would I find the courage to stand before those who sacrificed their time and money for me? How will they get reimbursed? I was also concerned with upholding my dignity before the Asian community. Maybe I would just escape to some remote island.

Come to think of it, my volunteers weren't supporting Paull Shin the politician, they were supporting the things I was committed to—good schools, more jobs, a better quality of life for all members of our diverse community. If my attempts and failures brought attention to these issues, I could try a thousand times, even just for the experience!

Once I diluted my obligation to win, I felt a huge burden evaporate, and determined not to allow one failure discourage me from the real objective.

I went out again to meet the evening rush hour. As my confidence grew, I became more aware of all the people telling me they had voted for me, or were on their way to vote for me. A bus with my face and name plastered on the side drove by, and trivialized the whole situation. Something about being confronted with my own face not only surprised me, it seemed to be teasing me.

After making a few more stops at busy intersections, I joined my family for a quiet dinner before going to the Howard Johnson Hotel for the election night reception.

By the time I arrived at the hotel, volunteers had set up a large screen TV, and were providing refreshments. The polls closed at eight p.m., and the tallies started right away in the district court office across the street. Results were reported to the hotel first, where the candidates were holding their receptions.

Volunteers, reporters, and visitors crowded every corner and hallway of the hotel. The news reported that there had been an alarming turnout rate in the polls this year, the highest in thirty years. Seventy percent of eligible voters had voted, in contrast to 1990. We also received news from the East Coast that Bill Clinton was comfortably ahead of George Bush in the presidential race.

Ron Lundberg, a respected teacher, friend and volunteer, was stationed at the court office and he called our room to relay the first set of results. The person who answered the phone announced to the room, "The results are in!"

The room fell silent with anticipation.

"Paull Shin, with 1,556 votes, is leading John Beck by 1 percent!"

An excited cheer exploded throughout the room, and seeped through the hallway.

In the primaries, I had trailed by as much as 14 percent, and had closed the gap to 2 percent in the end. Now I was ahead. It might have only been 1 percent, but it indicated progress.

Hearing an announcement of success from the beginning elevated everyone's expectations, and confidence liberated the crowded room. However, the close race left me feeling suffocated.

At nine-thirty, the next set of results came in.

"The Democratic candidate, Paull Shin, still in the lead by 4 percent, with 3,836 votes."

Another round of cheers escaped from my supporters, and I finally started to feel better, as if a grip around my neck had been loosened. Everyone seemed to be predicting my victory, and the excitement climaxed to the point of detonation.

By the third announcement at ten-thirty, my lead had increased to 7 percent.

Now we could safely congratulate each other. The reception room became a victory party, and the phones started to ring. My friend in Korea, former Congressman Hyunuk Kim supported me throughout the campaign, and called three times on the night of the election, to check on the status of the election.

At the final count, my lead had grown to about eight percent, and only the absentee ballots remained to be counted. Reporters rushed into the room to get a statement. There were hands to shake, calls to take, questions to answer. I locked myself in the bathroom to offer thanksgiving to the Lord, and returned to the crowd.

As the very first Korean-American to win a seat in the state House of Representatives, I had marked my place in history. Challenges awaited, but now I had some authority to make my voice heard.

thank you for thanking me

Despite the long day, I lie awake.

"What if the absentee ballots reverse the results?"

Exhilaration from the night, inspiration from encouragements, and my disbelief of victory chased away any hopes of rest.

Tired of just tossing in my bed, I went into my garage and found a large "Elect Paull Shin" sign. I turned it around, and wrote, "Thank You" on the other side. I wanted to thank all the voters for looking past superficial differences, and giving me a chance to serve my adopted country.

At around six o'clock in the morning, I held up my sign of gratitude at a busy intersection. Maybe it was the message on the sign or that I stood alone in the rain, but even more cars acknowledged my presence than they had the day before. Some people stepped out of their vehicles to shake my hand, while others brought me a hot cup of coffee. A few even gave me money.

"I've seen candidates waving signs to publicize their name before an election, but you're the first one to come back and thank us after you've won."

"Asians must have better manners."

"Shouldn't you be celebrating your victory?"

"You should get some rest!"

The Seattle Times reporter stopped by to take a picture that appeared not only in the next issue of the Times, but in newspapers around the country after it was picked up by the Associated Press. The publicity kept my phone ringing.

Anxious about the absentee ballots, I called the news station from a nearby telephone booth for the final count. John Beck, 17,158 votes, and Paull Shin, 20,523 votes.

I won. Was I dancing, smiling, or both? I didn't even feel the ground beneath my feet as I came out of the phone booth. Knowing that all the effort put into my campaign by friends, family, volunteers and strangers ended in success, sent me soaring.

Once the clock struck nine o'clock, the phone started ringing, and I didn't even get a chance to pinch myself to make sure I wasn't dreaming.

When I called my mother to tell her the results, she repeated a very familiar phrase:

"Your father would've been so proud!"

Whenever I returned to Geumchon, my grandmother used to say the same thing about my birth mother.

I returned to the streets to meet the evening rush hour, and held up my "Thank You" sign again.

A middle-aged man walked towards me, and said something very revelational.

"Thank you for thanking me!" he said.

We shook hands and parted, but his words remained. Every time someone thanked me, I wanted to return the gratitude.

After hearing his words, I found a renewed strength in my grip, and my sign felt like a feather blowing in the wind.

I also learned a very humbling lesson from John Beck, who had been my opponent during the campaign. He was the first person to come to my house to congratulate me on my victory. It made me wonder, "Would I have been able to congratulate him if I had lost?" He exemplified the value of the democratic experience and the rewards of a fair campaign.

In January of 1993, I was initiated into the House of Representatives as the first Korean-American representative. In the House Chamber, I spoke briefly to my new colleagues and my friends and family.

"What a miracle! I believed all the odds were against me, but I stand here as a privileged citizen of America. Where else could a street urchin dream of joining the House of Representatives? Where else would citizens vote for an inexperienced minority as their representative?

To all the individuals who volunteered their time and effort, I really don't know how to thank you—especially Donna, my wife, who volunteered her whole life to me. I would also like to thank my daughter, Alisa and son, Paull, who always stood by my side and helped me. And my adopted parents—I owe them my life, all my hopes and dreams, every-thing I've become.

By the grace of this country, I have been reborn. I feel I have more reasons to be grateful than anyone else in America. But I'm most grateful that I have been given this opportunity to express my gratitude. Now I can begin the main course of service. It's finally my turn to serve you.

Once again, I thank all those who trusted me, because without your votes, I would not be standing before you with my head up, shoulders squared, and my hands raised in victory."

Thirty-four years ago, after being thrown out of a segregated restaurant, I vowed, "Someday, I will serve you." I finally felt like I was in a position to fulfill this promise. I waited a long time, but I seized an opportunity I could not ignore.

In the thirty-four year gap, I prepared myself to face such a challenge, and at the same time, America progressed to the point where the mainstream could allow a minority to play a decisive role in the community.

Now I had no choice but to follow the difficult path I had chosen.

I just want to take the time to thank those who thank me.

"Thank you for thanking me!"

an eXodus for hope

"Are you sure you just got off the plane?" Donna asked me in disbelief. From Uzbekistan to Korea, and then a layover in Los Angeles before arriving in Seattle—I had been on and off planes for over 30 hours.

"Why do you ask?"

"I don't know. You look like someone who's ready to go to work."

Of course she was surprised. Donna reluctantly said goodbye to a man in despair—a man running away from his failure.

I had lost the race for Lieutenant Governor in 1996 by an extremely narrow margin. It was my second political loss in two years. I ran for a seat in the U.S. Congress, but that loss could be attributed to inexperience.

As Congressman Al Swift, from my congressional district,

was about to retire from his public service, he asked me to run for Congress as a Democratic candidate. I agreed without understanding the ramifications of a Federal race as opposed to a State election. I even found consolation in the fact that I had learned a lot from the experience.

Losing a second time, however, implicated the end of my political career. Because it was a state-wide campaign encompassing a population of about six million people, I worked harder than my previous elections, but my efforts were inevitably diluted.

But why only four percent? If the margin had been overwhelming or even just a reasonable ten percent, I might have accepted the loss more graciously, but running such a close battle kept me hoping until the very last absentee ballot was counted. The battle to the bitter end magnified my disappointment and left me completely exhausted.

I kept going over what I had done wrong, what I could have done differently. I blamed the situation, but above all, I blamed myself. If only I hadn't been so indecisive. If only I'd started my campaign a month sooner. No, not even that long, just a week, that's all I needed.

My supporters were gracious.

"We're always here if you need our help."

"Please keep fighting for our children."

"There's nothing wrong with losing. What's more important is that you learn from your mistakes. Washington State alone is twice as big as South Korea. Of over three million votes, to have lost by such a small margin is not a personal loss, but a victory for the community."

"Now that you have all the experience you need, you'll find your next victory very easily."

But words of consolation just sank to the bottom of my heart. There were optimists, and supporters, but what about the others?

"How could he lose at such a critical moment?"

"He'll never be able to show his face in the Asian community again!"

"He's hopeless! He's finished!"

To avoid public scrutiny, I sought the refuge of a remote corner in the Snoqualmie Mountains, and came out of hiding two days later to pack my bags.

What should I do now? I couldn't return to teaching as I had when I lost the Congressional race. What would my students think of a professor returning in failure for the second time? Maybe I should just retire and enjoy the rest of my life on the golf course. I couldn't live with the guilt of disappointing everyone who helped me, so I looked for an escape.

Samoa? Hawaii? Greece? Or a quiet, secluded lake? Not a single place came to mind where I felt I could release the grip of despair and hide from shame. Pastor Cheh, of the Korean church I attended advised me, "A place too quiet or extravagant increases loneliness. Why don't you reflect upon Korea's history of persecution and suffering?"

I looked out my window as the plane took off. Embroidered with lakes, decorated with mountains, colorful trees—a place filled with beauty—but the gossips and complaints drove me away in disgust.

The crowd in the Tashkent Airport in Uzbekistan seemed oblivious to the near freezing temperature inside. The extreme cold only aggravated my misery.

A Korean man greeted me, "You must be Dr. Paull Shin," he said. I'm Pastor Emmanuel Han. Pastor Cheh requested that I escort you." He took my bag and led me to a borrowed car—or, should I say freezer. I couldn't wait to get inside his home, but my frozen body was not so obliging.

Inside his home, Pastor Han told me how he came to be a missionary in Tashkent.

"I've made more money than I can spend, and I've done everything I desired. I thought I could ask for nothing more. Before my sixty-second birthday, I was diagnosed with cancer. I dropped everything and went to America to find a cure. Through medical care and prayer, the treatments were successful. Once I recovered, I devoted my life to God, and here I am."

"Don't you find it difficult living here by yourself?"

"My kids are all grown up, and my wife prefers to spend time with the grandchildren."

When we went to church the next Sunday, four grown men were holding chairs high above their heads. Among them was the doctor who lent his car to the pastor to pick me up at the airport. I couldn't stop from laughing at the sight of adults being punished like children.

Pastor Han explained, "Anyone caught speaking Russian instead of Korean in the church is punished regardless of age, gender, or profession."

When Japan annexed Korea in 1910, Korea became a Japanese colony, and Japan had legitimate rights to claim Koreans as Japanese citizens. Everyone knew that Korea was just a vanguard of Japanese imperialism, and anticipated the possibility of attacks in the neighboring countries. Japan, however, denied these allegations, and justified their invasion of Manchuria as an act of empowerment—ensuring that the Koreans, now Japanese citizens, living in Manchuria were not experiencing discrimination, or being treated unfairly. As a result, the Korean Freedom Fighters in Manchuria took refuge in Khabarovsk, Russia, and continued the independence movement.

In 1937, more than 170,000 Koreans were living in the Russian Far East, near Manchuria. Fearful that Japan might use the community of Koreans as a pretext for invading Russia, Stalin had the entire Korean community loaded into the cargo containers of trains and transported to the frozen wilderness of Kazakhstan and Uzbekistan, where he assumed the people would freeze to death, or die of starvation.

For over fifty years, the Korean language was strictly prohibited. Soon, even the first generation of refugees began to forget their own language. The bleak possibilities of producing second or third generation immigrants fluent in Korean never seemed to discourage Pastor Han, or impede his dedication.

In Almaty, the former capital city of Kazakhstan, I met Pastor Ki Ho Kim, a young man still in his thirties who had turned his back on personal ambitions and brought his wife and two children, ages seven and nine, to Kazakhstan as a missionary. He showed me the caves dug by Koreans to avoid the fatal winds blowing across the stark wilderness. Near the caves lie the graves of 42,000 Koreans who could not survive the tortures of starvation, or generate enough heat to thaw their frozen bodies during that first awful winter.

Looking across such an appalling sight brought a single word to summarize my horror: "Why?"

Why such persecution and suffering? Why Koreans?

I cried out of sympathy, and I cried out with rage.

When I looked a little further, I saw fields of cabbage and cotton. I could still sense the desperation of those trying to fertilize a barren land. These fields had not only been sown with sweat and hard work, but with the tears and devotion of a people refusing to allow difficult circumstances force them into despair.

That evening, a few elders shared their accounts of the tragic past at the pastor's home.

"I was only eight," an old woman said. "Our family broke through the frozen ground with stones to dig a cave as our shelter. We huddled closely together for warmth and tried to ignore the possibility of death."

"I still cringe at the thought of barely surviving the winters," another elder said. "When I remember the hunger and the cold, my body aches in protest."

In order to stay alive, everyone concentrated on working the fields to make some sort of living—children and adults alike. With so much work to be done, nobody had the time or energy to turn towards education. As a result, no one spoke either language very eloquently, but their testimonies were genuine and sincere, touching me with a sense of timeless pain.

Back in Tashkent, I met with about twenty, first generation survivors. Their memories may have faded over the years, but I knew the pain never subsided. Because they had gotten so accustomed to their agony, nobody burst into tears, or cried out with fury. Everyone shared a common experience, and no one considered their misfortune more heartbreaking than the others'.

"I remember seeing dead bodies everywhere. There wasn't a moment of silence. The nights echoed with cries of mourning, and we woke up to find more reasons to weep."

"That was only in the beginning. After a while we stopped crying for the dead. We could tell by the expressions on people's faces if someone in their family had died. I guess it seemed like nobody really had a right to grieve over something so universal. Who can measure the degree of sorrow for each loss? It was easier to go on with life."

"We dug," said a man. "That's what we did. We dug graves for the dead, and we kept digging to stay alive."

"My name is Cho, Sunah," a woman said. It took me a while to comprehend the significance of her name: ('Chosun' is the old name for Korea) Oh, Korea! "My father was a Korean freedom fighter, dedicated to seeing a liberated Korea, and always longed for Korea. Every time he called my name he could remember his homeland and be reminded of his mission."

...Chosunah...

**Lady Cho Sunah with a picture of her father
and fellow independence movement fighters**
Hope for a nation, encouragement for generations.
Their sacrifice and courage became the motivation that kept me fighting.

"I watched the Russian soldiers shoot my father and throw him out of a moving train," she continued. "My father, Cho, Myounghee, was a Korean nationalist who had fled to Manchuria in the 1920's to fight against Japanese imperialism. After the Japanese invasion of Manchuria in 1931, he escaped to Khabarovsk, where he was active in the anti-Japanese Korean Nationalist Movement as a freedom fighter, artist, and novelist."

Cho, Myounghee comforted his pain of separation and expressed his fervent love for his homeland, each time he called on his daughter. On the train to Kazakhstan, he had spoken out against the way the Koreans were being treated. He was killed instantly by a Russian soldier and thrown out of the moving train like a diseased corpse. Cho, Myounghee's remains may have turned to dirt in a nameless field, but the Russian soldier could not kill his spirit of resistance, because it shot through my own inadequacies like a burning arrow. I was re-ignited with a sense of responsibility and the warmth of love all over again. Now I could return to serve my country.

"I am ashamed to say that I came out here in despair to escape failure," I told the gathering. "Hearing about your experiences, and listening to how you overcame adversity makes me realize how insignificant my struggles are. I used to pride myself on the contributions I made to my adopted homeland, but now I realize how lazy and unproductive I've been. I will return to America encouraged by your perseverance, and motivated enough to disregard my failures. I too will follow your examples, and forbid myself to surrender."

This determination carried me through the multiple disappointments to follow, and fed me with the ability to turn my back to negativity.

As the captain announced our decent into Seattle, I looked out the window. When I had left Seattle, I had been too absorbed in my own pain to appreciate its beauty. As the plane's wings spread out over our destination, my heart opened to glide onto a runway full of hope.

Forty some years ago, a young boy full of dreams had looked out from an American cargo ship with excitement and anticipation, prepared to overcome obstacles. The same boy now entered an old man's heart to resurrect those dreams.

ame**r**ica

America, your name is New Land.
Land of opportunity,
Land of enduring hope.
Admired by the nations,
Desired by its people.

A symbol of freedom,
An answer to liberty.
Sheltering those defeated by oppression
Beckoning those burdened with despair,
Gathering all in a passionate embrace.

In Your magnificence,
You offer hope.
In Your splendor,
You provide opportunity.
Too often misrepresented,
Too easily misunderstood,
Strong and mighty,
Yet humble in spirit.

Who dares to attack?
Who dare threatens,
To inflict pain and suffering?

What caused these tears I see,
Flowing from your eyes?
Flooding the streams and rivers,
Into the cities and homes.

The ends of the earth would not be too far,
My life not too precious,
To defend and sustain
Your unprecedented honor,
Till justice rings true throughout the land.

The New Land—your name is America.
Land of blessings, Land of prosperity,
Protected by the seal,
"In God We Trust".

Just as peace and tranquility
Follow the storm,
A radiant sunrise
Clears the darkness.
Restoration begins as we unite.

You reign in our hearts,

Now stronger than ever.

Drawing all nations

To marvel at your grace.

a glimmer of hope

"So, I hear you're going to run against me."

"Well, I'm considering the possibility—assessing myself, and evaluating the consequences. But when I make a decision, I'll let you know."

In the process of finalizing my decision, I wanted to pay a courtesy call to the incumbent Senator who represented my district, not only as an opponent, but as a former colleague in the House of Representatives. I respected her as a politician, and wanted to maintain good relations.

She warned me of a difficult campaign that lie ahead, but after much contemplation, I concluded that the benefits outweighed the costs, and decided to challenge myself.

Before launching my campaign, I thanked God for renewing my sense of hope through the example of Cho Sunah, and promised to give the campaign my best efforts. I set some specific goals for myself in hopes of leading a more successful and productive campaign.

1. I hired a young, competent campaign manager. I found that the older you get, the more you revert to conservative ideals. I needed someone energetic, someone who could overcome unexpected situations, and someone willing to take risks.

2. Organized a campaign steering committee to form strategies and make plans. I asked personal friends, college acquaintances, church friends, city and county council members, mayors, former politicians, and even the current Snohomish County Executive.

3. Sought the help of the community through endorsements. Not only would I gain financial assistance, I would also secure their support. The Machinist Union, Washington State Teacher's association, Washington State Labor Council, Washington State Fire Fighters, Washington State Teamster's Union, Nurse Association, Trial Lawyer's Association, Dental Association, Washington State Optometrists' Association, Real Estate Associations, and Washington State Patrol were some of the groups who trusted and endorsed my campaign.

4. The Washington State Korean Community also organized the Paull Shin Support Group with Michael Chung as the Chairman, and Kwangsuk Kim as the Vice Chairman. They helped raise campaign funds, assisted in increasing voter registration, organized rally groups and recruited volunteers to help with the campaign.

5. I wanted to personally meet every single voter. Everyone deserved to receive the full impact of my determination, and I was responsible for providing them with the opportunity to witness my dedication. I made a commitment to knock on every door in my district.

Doorbelling is an important tactic in any campaign; in my case, it was absolutely essential. I realized it was the only way to communicate with all the potential supporters. Especially in the Lieutenant Governor race, the large coverage area really restricted me from distributing my efforts equally. I was literally running around between the borders, trying to cover as much ground as possible. I didn't have enough money or time to effectively publicize myself in eastern Washington, which was the most conservative and least ethnically diverse region of the state, and the area where I needed the most exposure. In eastern Washington, I was a foreigner who had no business running for public office. In their minds I should be selling groceries in the international district or cooking in an Asian restaurant. Voters didn't know me, and had I met more of them face to face, more people would have reacted to me as a person, not just an Asian face they saw on TV or parades. Voters were unfamiliar with my name, and uncomfortable with my face.

My main objective of knocking on every door was to develop a more intimate relationship with all my constituents. I learned the importance of a single vote, and I knew I had to earn each vote through hard work. For this campaign, I decided not to rely on the media, because I considered it running an institutional campaign. I needed a personal campaign, building personal relationships, and making individual contact.

Reaching every home would be difficult, but not impossible. I started by carefully studying the district divisions. There were 138 precincts within the district, and I had less than ten months to accomplish my goal.

Unfortunately, with the exception of a few apartment compounds and condominium units, the 21st district covers a very prosperous area of big homes and spacious lots, where residents enjoy elaborate landscaping, but hopelessly looking up to a house at the top of a steep hill never helped me reach the doorstep. No matter how difficult my circumstance became, my resolution never faltered. Results provided comfort, and positive reactions diminished my pain.

When I approached the door with humility, voters accepted me much more willingly.

"Hello, my name is Paull Shin. I am a Democratic candidate for the State Senate. America is my adopted country. I have been blessed so much in this country, and I want to show my appreciation by serving the state. Would you please help me to serve you?"

Most of the time, the response was positive.

"You've got our votes."

"You climbed that hill to meet me? I'll definitely vote for you!"

"You're the first political candidate to pay a personal visit to my home!"

"You mean you came all the way here for a single vote?"

"You look honest enough. I think I'll vote for you."

"Just because you came here on a rainy day, I'll vote for you!"

"You must be exhausted in this heat! Yes! I'll vote for you!"

Every now and then someone would say, "I'm a Republican, but I'll vote for you anyway," and I would feel especially gratified.

Some votes took much more sacrifice than others. "Beware of Dog" signs really slowed me down, but never stopped me even after several attacks.

"I'm so sorry. Our dog is very protective ...but we'll definitely vote for you now."

Earning one more vote compensated the wound, and proved that dogs really could become man's best friend.

As always, I preferred the physical wounds to verbal abuse. Some were indirect in their rejection: "How do you expect to get elected in this district?" Others came right to the point: "We don't vote for Orientals!" On several occasions I had the door slammed in my face with comments such as, "Don't bother ever coming to our house again!" and I would silently stand on the doorstep, regaining my composure and remembering how it felt years ago to be turned away from a house by an angry house wife. At least now no one was chasing me away with a broom or slapping me across the face.

There was always another voter waiting to open their door.

In any situation, I gave maximum respect to my constituents, because a confrontation would be much too beneficial for my opponent, and most of the hostile residents slammed the door in my face before I had a chance to defend myself.

One day, however, a man in his mid-sixties really challenged my self-control.

"There are too many Orientals in this country! Why don't you go back home? We don't need you here."

I felt my nails digging into my palms, trying to control my temper. I realized I needed to protect my campaign before my pride. If I harmed this man in any way to appease my anger now, I would have to face eager newspaper headlines tomorrow. The last thing I wanted was to pick up the newspaper tomorrow and see a headline on the front page, "Senate Candidate Assaults Constituent."

"Sir, let me clarify something." I said, as calmly as I could, "This is my home. I have been in this country for the last forty-four years, and I've been paying taxes for the last forty-three years. I served this country as a soldier in Germany for two years and in the state legislature for two years. I love young people, so I taught in college for thirty-one years, and became a board member for different youth organizations such as Boy Scouts, and the YMCA. I'm also involved in other charity foundations, and even helped establish a few organizations in this community. My wife and children are all American citizens. So, you see, this is my home. You're telling me to go home, but where do you expect me to go?"

He must have been moved by my response because his expression softened, and I continued.

"This land was built upon the hopes and dreams of immigrants. According to history, neither of us belongs here. Since your ancestors came here first, why don't you take the lead and return home first? Then I'll follow you."

Guilt replaced his animosity, and remorse changed once again to affirmation. He put his hands on my shoulders and said, "My friend, I'll vote for you. Not only that, I'd like to help you."

That day, I not only earned an extra vote, but I made a life-long friend. Ted joined me as a doorbelling partner, walking by my side, and shamelessly adding, "Vote for him. He's a good man." He called on his own acquaintances for support, and made a substantial financial contribution himself.

My encounter with Ted gave me the hope that ignorance could be converted into awareness, and that those who stood against me might one day stand beside me as a friend. Knowing that initial opposition could turn into an alliance encouraged me to walk towards the next door.

A few months into my campaign, I received a call from The Seattle Times reporter. He said, "I understand you walk a lot."

"I walk everyday," I replied.

"How many homes have you visited so far?"

"Oh, I would guess about 14,000 homes…"

It took him a while to absorb the reality of the number, especially because I replied so casually.

Once he recovered from the shock he asked, "Can I come and walk with you?"

"You are most welcome to join me."

The next day, he brought a photographer and the three of us walked as I had been doing, but after two hours, they gave up.

"I can't even keep up with you for two hours! How do you walk eleven hours everyday? How can you walk for so long?" he asked.

I jokingly smiled, pat my legs and said, "You see these? These were made in Korea."

In the next Sunday paper, I read a story about an immigrant from Korea, adopted by an American soldier, who worked hard to earn a GED and eventually a PhD. He wanted to return the blessings he received in the United States by offering himself as a public servant. He would leave home around nine a.m. as his wife waves to send him off to meet and greet his constituents. When he returns late at night, she is waiting with a bucket of warm water and Epsom salt to nurse his bleeding feet. Now this is the dedication and commitment we want to see in our politicians!

I walked an average of over eleven hours a day for nine long months. I visited 29,000 homes and walked through four pairs of shoes. In the last month before the election, I stood next to highways and busy intersections waving signs.

I didn't want to hide my face in shame, or give voters a false impression of my image. I wanted to be seen and evaluated as a person, and trusted as a fellow citizen, not an unapproachable politician. I sought to break the superficial barriers of race. I wanted people to know that despite my color, we shared common aspirations—for our family, our community, our country. Through hard work, I overcame my feelings of inadequacy, and hard work communicated through all barriers.

As I trudged from house to house, I was struck by the irony of my situation. Since coming to America, I had tried to extinguish all memories of my degrading experiences on the streets of Korea. I had come to America to change my life, but here I was voluntarily choosing to become what I had promised to never allow myself to be again—a beggar. In Korea I had begged for food. Now in America, I was begging for votes.

infectious attitudes

Once the excitement of victory dissipated, the guests started to find their way home. In the safety of my own room, I thanked God for stimulating my courage, reviving my strength, and sustaining my motivation. One last question remained in my mind: "Where do I go from here?" In my determination to win, I had forgotten the burden of victory.

As I had done in previous races, I spent Election Day waving signs on the streets, and enjoyed a quiet dinner with my family. The only difference was that this time my body felt really sore. I hated to admit it, but I could really feel the impact of age.

After dinner, we headed to the campaign headquarter at the Lynnwood Embassy Suites to await the results.

To everyone's surprise, I took an early lead that only increased over time. The final count was 58%−42%, which constitutes a landslide victory.

For many justifiable reasons, my opponent felt no initial competition from me. Early in the campaign, <u>The Seattle Times</u>, the largest newspaper in the state, had labeled my opponent the "Unsinkable Titanic." As the incumbent Senator, she was a popular and well-respected veteran politician who had also served on the City Council, as a Mayor, and in the House of Representatives.

Once she witnessed her precarious situation, her campaign team took a different approach. As money poured in, her campaign increased their ads and hired telemarketing companies to solicit votes in an attempt to question the legitimacy of my candidacy. The telemarketer would begin by asking, "Who do you plan to vote for in the upcoming election?" If the answer was my opponent, the conversation ended with a polite "thank you", but if they answered, "Paull Shin," the caller would ask, "Why?" and proceed to change the person's mind. "Do you really want an inexperienced man to represent you?"

I received such phone calls in my own home, but I resolved to maintain a positive campaign, and found it much more effective. People seemed to appreciate my approach; some even thanked me for not retaliating and preserving the integrity of the campaign. I felt voters deserved an explanation, so we ran a half page add in <u>The Seattle Times</u>. The ad helped restore my credibility, and convinced voters that their opinion of me should remain unaffected by my opponent's media blitz. In the end, the press called me the "iceberg" that sank the Titanic.

In the past, I always felt restrained by the fact that I did not feel embraced in a predominantly white society. I made a promise to serve this country, and was determined to contribute my part as a proud, grateful citizen, but I always underestimated my influential capacity. There was a time when encountering another Asian was very rare, but blending in or conforming to the visible trends was impossible. In 1955, the "land of equality" was not exactly hospitable to all. However, in less than fifty years, America has adapted to the demands of a population growing ethnically and culturally more diverse each year. In an increasing number of cities, we are approaching the point where no one is a majority and everyone is a member of this country with common goals and aspirations.

If there ever was a time, I believe now is the time when ethnic barriers should become less and less visible, to facilitate this transitional period in America. Most people shy away from differences, and prefer to remain within the boundaries of their comfort zone. Holding onto obsolete labels, and remembering irrelevant data prevents us from accommodating a progressive nation.

My daughter, Alisa, came home from school in tears one day, so I wanted to comfort her.

"Why are you crying?"

"I hate school! I'm never going back to school again!"

It was a familiar phrase coming from a child in elementary school, but I asked anyways, "What happened?"

"The kids at school were calling me shrimp eyes!"

As a father, I wanted to get the names of all the kids and teach them a lesson, but I knew irrationality would only aggravate the situation.

Instead I told her, "Lisa, the other kids just don't appreciate the beauty of your eyes. In your eyes, I see a perfect blend of Caucasian and Asian qualities."

I tried to give her confidence in her uniqueness, and emphasized the importance of individuality. Lisa looks a lot more "American" than I or most other Asians, but she still suffered for her minor differences.

Over the years, I've been exposed to many aspects of discrimination, social and racial. Through my experiences, I learned the futility of fighting or battling each confrontation. As I started to feel sorry for myself, bitterness and hatred set in, bringing out emotions that I wanted to eliminate. Blaming others never helped. I sought out ways to cope with the pain, and developed resilience to negativity. Self-actualization finally concluded an endless search for approaches, and absorbed years of disappointment.

Upon my arrival in the United States, I assumed the identity of Paull Shin, but underneath, I was a nobody trying to become an American, and very unsuccessful in my endeavor. Everything I tried to run away from eventually caught up to me in the form of emotional insecurity. Many suicides result from obscure identities. Sadly, statistics show that Korean-American girls have the highest suicide rate in the United States. Going beyond racial boundaries and cultural limitations, I established security in who I considered myself to be, without abandoning my heritage. Mirrors are a constant reminder of my origin, and even if I changed my appearance, I couldn't deny the life pumping through my body.

As a State Senator, in 2002, I sponsored legislation to remove the term "Oriental" as it refers to people, from Washington State law. Asian-Americans identify "Oriental" as a pejorative term with negative connotations, regardless of intentions. It was my good friend Ted, who suggested I sponsor the legislation because he called me "oriental" when I first met him at his door during my campaign.

The law, as currently written, now replaces the obsolete, pejorative term, "Oriental," with the more politically correct term, "Asian," in all state laws and codes. In a country striving for political correctness, this terminology was immediately endorsed and implemented as the official reference for Asian-Americans by the United States Congress.

With this success, I received an invitation to speak at the Southern Christian Leadership Conference in Kansas City, Missouri, and when Martin Luther King III greeted me, he said, "If my father were alive, he would be the first to congratulate you and thank you."

I believe that everyone has a right to define themselves, rather than allowing stereotypes and preconceived notions to determine identities. Building idiosyncrasies through personal goals makes life more than just tedious routines. In an exploration of self-discovery, there are no irrelevant experiences, or unnecessary factors. My determination to pursue my dream provoked condemnation from peers, but I learned to distinguish between sincerity and hypocrisy through my own mistakes. How can we transport "I have a dream" from the vision of one great man, to the hearts of every American?

I witnessed the importance of a life driven by "hopes and dreams". Hopes and dreams secure futures when applied with hard work. Such a statement may seem vague or redundant, and the combination of "hopes and dreams" has become a cliché, trivializing the significance and necessity. Despite similar aspirations, diverse characters designate a different course appropriate for the individual.

"Survival of the fittest" is not just a theory of evolution, it determines the magnitude of our existence, and instills hard work ethics. I admit that in the past, I anticipated failure to force greater exertion. I wanted to assure that I tried my best, and have no regrets, but my efforts were exhausting. Instead of competing for superiority, I want to generate an attitude of encouragement and unity. My Asian birth and American upbringing provides me with the ability to function as a bridge between two continents.

With letters of recommendations from five U.S. Senators, two Governors, and six Congressmen, I became a candidate for the position of American Ambassador to Korea. After an extensive elimination process, including a thorough investigation of my background, I was accepted as one of the finalists, which required an interview with a panel of State Department officials.

I was asked very pertinent questions on trade and diplomacy, and towards the end of the interview, one person asked, "Dr. Shin, suppose you became the Ambassador, and there is a conflict between United States and Korea. Which side would you take?" It was a hypothetical situation, but I couldn't help but question its motive. I had no room for escape, so I sat in silence for a moment, considered my obligations, and began my response.

"Thank you for asking me that question. Now let me tell you how I feel deep inside. Korea is my motherland. She bore me, giving me life, blood, and heritage. America is my fatherland, where I received love, family, education, and economic opportunities. This is where I discovered myself. When my mother and father are in disagreement, it would be in my best interest to find a way for them to reconcile and get along. You're asking me to choose between my mother and father? Let me ask you, which side would you choose?"

My patriotism towards America remained unquestionable, but I still feel loyal to Korea. I had tried to renounce Korea, only to find that my rejection led to an identity crisis. Before we criticize the perpetrators of racism, we must examine our own reactions— "How objectively am I evaluating the situation?"—and discover ways to facilitate unity. I believe racial discrimination is not inherent, but develops from a lack of understanding.

In order to facilitate awareness, I sponsored legislation to help establish the month of May as Asian/Pacific Islander's Heritage Month in the state of Washington, to encourage mutual awareness and understanding. In order to get along in a multi-cultural, interdependent society, we need more knowledge to better prepare ourselves. Working with cooperation and conciliation proves to be much more effective than conflict and confrontation. As a result, the United States Congress also adopted legislation to designate the month of May as Asian/Pacific Islander's Heritage Month.

America has been represented through many different metaphors: the quilt, the crucible, a salad bowl, and even Marilyn Monroe. Perhaps the most prevalent reference is the old paradigm of the melting pot. This illustration, however, leaves room for a dangerous misconception. I feel that complete assimilation is just as threatening as segregation. Problems may not be as evident, but dissolving individuality is a suicidal attempt to create harmony. Pride in our individuality allows us to transcend vain structures, and disregard the levels of inequality.

I personally like the idea of America as a beautiful tapestry with all the different colors and threads delicately woven together to show dedication and commitment. America has never been commended for its simplicity. And in the case of this art work, the more complex, the more beautiful the masterpiece. A single thread is weak, but the intricacy of a tapestry provides reinforcement. The full potential of America comes into power when everyone exercises their democratic rights, which entails that we eliminate fatalistic attitudes.

Racial discrimination encountered today can be much more subtle and debilitating than fifty years ago. The surviving precedence of implied inferiority incapacitates even more than blatant segregation. I used to consider myself a "colored" man, and applied myself according to popular expectations. However, I realized that I was restricting myself even before anyone imposed any barriers. I believe in maintaining confidence in our identities by exploring ways to enhance and accommodate the societies we inhabit. Minor contributions magnify upon impact when we discredit stereotypes and participate as a nation. Just as a small spark creates a fire, we are fully capable of enriching America through what we have to offer.

My greatest hope lies in the future. Not my own, but in those willing to take advantage of me—my experiences and my struggles. I don't have the ability to force desires, but I yearn to see representation. Recognizing potential always manages to awaken and re-ignite an undying passion to reach out and empower. I feel a responsibility to apply my strengths and weaknesses, to hold hands with the future.

Echoing Mother Theresa,

"I know I have not done any great things.

I have only done small things.

But every small thing I did, I did with great love."

Not to anticipate my own death, but I have already decided what I want my tombstone to read, "Here lays a man who found himself in two cultures and found the world."

Many, many years ago, a nameless American soldier pulled me up into his truck. The moment marked the beginning of a transformation, allowing me to abandon Shin Hobom, to become Paull Shin. But in the process of constructing a new identity for myself, I lost something precious. Just as the soldier offered his hand to young Hobom, so would I, years later, reach out to the boy I had once rejected and lift him back into my life.

The story that I have told in this book has been a part of that process of self-acceptance.

under construction

I turned my back to familiarity...
Seeking freedom, escaping oppression,
Imagining the rewards of transformation.
Over mountains, across the ocean,
An impossible journey towards assimilation.

Withstanding pressure required desperate measures...
The first few years deaf and speechless,
Years of caution countless.
Obstacles discouraging, I must confess,
Especially in times of extreme loneliness.

Blindly searching through a bleak horizon...
Oblivious to the tears at my feet,
Already flowing as a stream complete.
Too soon to quit, resisting defeat,
Strongly believing, "I can't be beat."

I stretch my stiffened knees with great difficulty,
Squint my eyes to face reality.

I'm extremely encouraged to see...
A forest of potential populating this nation,
All grown beyond recognition.
With my youth in dissipation,
What can I offer the next generation?

As a farmer sowing a garden of treasures...
I plant dreams in the hearts of those,
Refusing limits as I once chose.
Infectious attitudes battling foes
Eliminate ignorance till everyone knows.

Before the Washington State Capitol Building?
Hoping that many will follow and do many greater things than
I could ever imagine.